3 Things I Wouldn't Do for Money

and Other Ruminations from Suburbia

3 Things I Wouldn't Do for Money

and Other Ruminations from Suburbia

Vivian Charlton

iUniverse, Inc.
New York Bloomington

3 Things I Wouldn't Do for Money
And Other Ruminations from Suburbia

iUniverse books may be ordered through booksellers or by contacting:

iUniverse
1663 Liberty Drive
Bloomington, IN 47403
www.iuniverse.com
1-800-Authors (1-800-288-4677)

Because of the dynamic nature of the Internet, any Web addresses or links contained in this book may have changed since publication and may no longer be valid. The views expressed in this work are solely those of the author and do not necessarily reflect the views of the publisher, and the publisher hereby disclaims any responsibility for them.

ISBN: 978-1-4502-4674-3 (sc)
ISBN: 978-1-4502-4675-0 (ebook)

Library of Congress Control Number: 2011906775

Printed in the United States of America

iUniverse rev. date: 06/15/2011

This book is dedicated to Vivian.
Her love of life and laughter
will live in our hearts forever.

Contents

Introduction:
In Memory of Vivian

Maybe, as a kind of introduction to these stories, I can try to give a sense (from a little brother's perspective) of what sort of person Viv was. I know I don't really need to, because the voice that goes so clearly through all these stories is her voice; the nutty ideas that come spilling out of her characters are so much her ideas; and the stories are in some cases so slightly fictionalized that the reader will come away from these stories knowing her perfectly well without my help.

I'm thinking right now of when we were growing up in Berkeley. My sister Phil was the oldest. Viv was a year younger, and I was several years younger. I can tell many stories of her wild youth. Anyway, it seemed very wild then, though in fact, it was all very innocent by today's standards. For example, there was her boyfriend, Pete. I was one of the stars among the other kids in the neighborhood because I knew Pete. Some of his admirable qualities were: (1) he drove a big four-cylinder Indian motorcycle; (2) he had a .45 that he showed us kids once; and (3) his name was in the paper once when the police broke up a big fight. He was actually a pretty nice guy, just a little bit wild.

As Viv was. She fooled around so much she flunked out of high school and got all Fs in her final term. So she was sent to this very expensive school for rich flunk-outs, and our father laid down the law. No going out. Period. Every evening after dinner, she would go to her room. The door would be closed, and she would *study*. Well, maybe she studied for half an hour a night, which was certainly more than she had ever studied before; in fact, it was enough to get her all As, and she was the valedictorian of her graduating class. (I think you can also hear a lot of intelligence, if perhaps considerable recklessness, in the voice of these stories.) But after that half hour, she opened her ground-floor bedroom window and jumped out to go off with her friends. She had a wonderful time while my mother and Phil and I sat home in absolute terror that our father would discover that she was gone. But he never did.

Viv was a very outgoing, social person. She liked people. She also liked dogs. She maybe endured cats. That was the extent of her liking for living things. Everything else that moved was terrifying to her. The problem was I was the opposite. I sometimes didn't care all that much about people, but I loved every living, moving, wriggling, undulating thing, and I dragged home every snake or spider or whatever else I found and spent my time making cages and containers for all my pets.

I remember once I was out in the backyard when Viv came running out, her face white, and shouted, "There's a dinosaur in the kitchen!"

I went running in enthusiastically, thinking, *What do you feed a dinosaur? How big a cage will I need?* Viv gestured toward the cabinet under the sink. I looked in and very disappointedly found one of my fairly tiny lizards had escaped.

She was not always irresponsible about her education. After her successful graduation from high school, she of course decided to go to college. She started at UC Berkeley, but that was not to her liking. She got university catalogs from all over the country and studied them avidly. She was not looking to see which university had the strongest program in philosophy or theoretical physics. She was looking to see which university had the highest percentage of men and the lowest percentage of women. The University of Oregon had way more men than women, so that's where she went and where she met her husband, Bob.

When Bob got his BA, they moved to Southern California, and Viv got a number of wacky jobs (which show up in some of these stories) helping to put her husband through graduate art college. After that, she was involved in raising her children. But as they became more independent and she began to have more time on her hands, she suddenly remembered how much fun she had had going out and meeting new people and dealing with the public when she was working. So she got involved in local politics, and then she went to law school, serious about her education for the first time, and wrote the best briefs in her class. Who knows where she might have gone? But by then, the marriage was breaking up, and she was going to have to support herself. She had not worked for years, but in her usual confident and undaunted way, she got a real estate license and fell into the job she was made for, going through houses, which she had always loved, and dealing with the public, which she had always enjoyed. She quickly became a top salesperson.

As eventually happens to all of us, she got older, retired, and settled down to enjoy her grandchildren. But sitting at home was not her way. She joined a breakfast club, a group of sociable people with their own wild stories to tell, who met once a week for breakfast, and then she joined a writing club that met on another day of the week. Writing was what, in the back of her mind, she had always most wanted to do, but somehow, the busyness of life had kept her from it. Here was an interesting group of creative people, sharing their creations with each other, getting encouragement and feedback. She was nearly eighty years old and in her element.

It was around this time she was diagnosed with multiple myeloma. Except for two very special works at the end, you won't find of a breath of this in the stories; she was much too positive for that. But in the years she doggedly fought this illness, working on her stories and sharing them with an audience became one of the most important things in her life. I think, in a very literal way, she lived for her writing.

Norman Lavers

1. *What's Your Sign?*

The only people I've ever heard of who even talked about astrological signs were the morons who sat on bar stools asking people what their signs were. So I consulted an encyclopedia, and the section under "Astrology" tells me that one's temperament and destiny depend upon the zodiacal constellation under which he is born. With our knowledge of medicine today, we know the date a woman gives birth can vary from the expected due date, sometimes crossing zodiacal lines. Does this mean the poor person waiting inside may have to keep changing his personality back and forth until his mother decides when she will give birth?

I happen to be very closely involved in this subject, for you see, I am one of a pair of identical twins. We were named Vivian and Velma, and we were due August 22. We knew nothing about the zodiac until our mother went to a lecture one day, and of course, we had no choice but to sit there in her womb and listen. We were amazed by what we learned. Since August

22 was our due date, that meant we were Leos, and we laughed when we heard all the adjectives describing our personalities. Leos are described as ambitious, courageous, dominant, strong willed, positive, independent, self-confident—the list is so long you would have to be a Leo just to get through it. And there was also the dark side—we were pompous, bossy, intolerant, patronizing .... It sounded like so much fun we could hardly wait to get out and start annoying people.

As we approached the twenty-second of August, we had grown so much there was barely enough room for the both of us. Neither of us would give an inch as we tried to assume the dominant position in the womb.

On the big day, Mother refused to stay home. She and my father had been invited to a bridge party, and she said she felt fine and had plenty of time to go to the party and then check in at the hospital afterwards. Velma was mad.

"Don't you see what could happen?" she said. "If she doesn't let us come out before midnight, we'll be Virgos!"

I thought back to that lecture, and all I could remember about Virgos was that they were dependable, orderly, neat ... This sounded so boring I had quit listening. I sure didn't want to miss our due date for *that*.

The hours passed, and Mother kept sitting there playing cards. So she was feeling fine, was she? We'd take care of that. We began kicking and pounding on her until she was crying out in pain. Father pulled her up and dragged her out of the room.

By the time we got to the hospital, it was 11:50. How could she do this to us?

We heard the doctor say, "I think one of them is about to come out." And that was the last thing I heard for a few moments, as without warning, Velma turned and hit me as hard as she could and I was temporarily stunned. I lost consciousness for a moment, and the next thing I knew, I was all alone.

I struggled and managed to push myself out into the brightly lit room, but it was too late. The clock on the wall said 12:05, and I knew what Velma had done. She knew there was only time enough for one of us to make it before midnight. And now, thanks to her treachery, she would grow up as a voluptuous vixen named Velma. And I was now destined to be virtuous Vivian, class valedictorian.

But something rather odd had come over me. I didn't seem to mind it as much as I thought. In fact, I looked over at Velma and thought how loudly she was crying. What a lot of racket over nothing! I think she just liked all the attention.

They finished with the measuring and weighing, and a nurse put a diaper on me. I hoped she did a better job than she had done on Velma. Her diaper wasn't even folded correctly.

2. *Going Incognito*

There were actually two times in my life that I tried to be someone else, once with good results, once with bad.

Let's start with the bad so I can get rid of it. I was in high school, the eleventh grade to be precise. My sister and brother and I always got good grades in school—not because we were so smart, but because my father was very strict. Education came first in our house, and my father pretty much gave us two choices: do our homework or die.

There was a group of kids at my school that I admired and envied. They always seemed to do what they wanted and get away with it. One day, one of the girls told me they were ditching school the next day to go to Stinson Beach, which was located just north of San Francisco and was a popular hangout for delinquent kids. I had never been there.

"But how will you get back in class?" I asked her. "My mother would never write me an excuse."

She looked at me to see if I was kidding. "So write your own," was the reply.

The next day, with my bathing suit stuffed into my book bag, I met the kids on a corner just north of school, and we took off.

It was great, and my conscience didn't bother me a bit. In fact, knowing I should be in school kind of added a little spice. Several of the kids seemed surprised to see me there and said they had thought I was a snob. I was in heaven. I had finally been accepted by the misfits and losers!

When I got home, my mother was in the kitchen starting dinner, so I slipped into her room and sat at her desk. There was her lavender notepaper. I took several sheets. I also took a paper that she had signed and went to my room to practice her signature. I wrote a note about what a bad head cold Vivian had and how I thought it best to keep her home for a day.

The next morning, I handed my note in at the office and was given a slip to get back into class. How easy!

That was just the beginning of weeks and weeks where I got tanner, but my homework got briefer and I got some pretty low test scores. One of my teachers was concerned enough by my sudden change in behavior that he took me aside and asked kindly if I was having trouble at home. I felt like saying, "Not yet."

The fun of being my mother and writing one gracious excuse after another might have gone on all term but for a dentist appointment I had. My mother gave me a note to get out of class, and without thinking, I turned it in. The office got their first look at a real note from my mother. The next day, I was called to the vice principal's office. I knew this was not going to be a good day when I entered the room and saw my father sitting there. On the top of the vice principal's desk were spread out several lavender pieces of paper.

The vice principal told my father that I was in danger of flunking most of my classes. From that day on, I was grounded, so even I could figure out that those days at the beach hadn't been worth it.

But just to let you know there can be a happy outcome to being deceitful, and once in a while, cheaters do prosper, let me tell you what I pulled just two years later.

I was now a freshman at UC Berkeley, and one day, I read in the paper that Gregory Peck was at the Geary Theater in San Francisco starring in Gaslight. I was a huge fan of his, so I phoned the theater and said I wrote a column for the *Daily Californian*, which was the campus newspaper. Of course, I didn't, but this seemed an easy way to get inside. I said I would like to interview Mr. Peck, and I was told to come to the stage door at intermission that Sunday. There was quite a mob of fans there, but when I identified myself, they had to make way for me, and I was let in and taken to his dressing room. I had a notebook with me and some thoughts about possible questions. But when I sat just a few feet away from him, looked into his handsome face, and heard that trademark rumbling voice of his, I almost went into a trance.

Fortunately for me, he was a graduate of Cal and had been on their rowing team; he began telling me funny stories of things that had happened during some of their races. So he actually did most of the talking, while I sat there gazing up at him, trying not to drool like an idiot.

In about ten minutes, his manager said the interview was over. Mr. Peck stood up and actually shook my hand and thanked me for coming. I somehow stumbled back out of the stage door and found my way home.

I admit that my first bit of deceit was potentially harmful, but I think even my father might agree that my second lie was just downright creative. It did no harm to Gregory Peck, and it sure gave me a lifelong memory.

3. *Playing Walter Mitty*

I guess the thing I like most about myself is the curiosity I've always had that causes me to volunteer to do all sorts of things, whether I'm qualified or not. This has led to a few disasters, but on the whole, it has added a lot of spice to my life.

An early example would be when I was a freshman at UC Berkeley. I saw a flyer announcing that the drama department was holding auditions for a musical. So I cut my next class to go over and stand in a very long line. One by one, we walked across the stage to the piano and sang a short song. When I finished, I was waved over to the group that was accepted. The odd part of this story is the fact that I am not a singer. I can carry a tune, but I don't have a great voice, or even a good one. I later found out that the director needed a lot of people for the chorus but didn't want divas who would try to drown everyone out. He just wanted people who could stay on key and blend in. But I didn't know this at the time, so why did I even try out? I was just curious to see if I could do it.

But not all of my little tryouts worked out as well. I remember when I was sixteen, an underground parking garage had just opened in San Francisco. It was summer vacation, and a couple of my friends were going over to apply for jobs as parking attendants. I had just gotten my driver's license that week, and my cautious parents had not yet even let me take the car out alone. But I thought, *Why not?* and went with my friends to apply. When it was my turn to demonstrate my driving skills, a man told me to get into a car that a customer had just dropped off and to park it down on the fourth level. He got in on the passenger side. I did very well going round and round down two levels and was feeling pretty cool. But then I cut a corner too sharply and smashed the right front fender into a post. The man jumped out, came around the car, and pushed me aside so he could take over the wheel. He drove immediately to the bottom level where there was a body shop to take care of just such emergencies. When I got back up to street level, the manager told me to go home and learn how to drive.

Growing up didn't change my desire to occasionally venture into unknown situations. When the O.J. murders occurred, I was fascinated by the trial and taped it anytime I couldn't be home. One day, I read about a cruise being put together just for the O.J. trial watchers. The ship would go to Ensenada and back, and among the guests would be many of the people who were having their fifteen minutes of fame by testifying. Also invited were many of the lawyers who were picking up extra money by appearing on the nightly television recaps of the trial. The article also said that there would be a mock trial during this cruise, and any passengers who wanted to take part could submit their scripts when they boarded. That was all I needed. I bought my ticket and boarded the ship with an eight-page closing argument for the prosecution.

Two hundred people showed up for the O.J. tour, and they put us in a separate part of the ship from the regular passengers. All day, there were O.J. discussions going on in various rooms led by the guest speakers. To show how minor these guests were, one popular speaker was the limo driver who drove O.J. to the airport the night of the murders. We were such trial junkies we didn't even get off the ship at Ensenada, just stayed aboard attending more discussion groups.

Sunday night, on our return trip, they had the mock trial. The passenger who played the judge wore a huge Judge Ito mask, and all two hundred of us squeezed into the lounge being used as a courtroom. It was a very festive occasion, and the bar service was kept very busy. My closing argument was selected, so I played the part of the prosecuting attorney. I figured it would be a slam dunk, as everyone I had talked to all weekend thought O.J. was guilty. In fact, every one of the scripts handed in was for the prosecution, and they had a difficult time finding someone to play the defense attorney. They finally coaxed one of the men into doing it. It was like no trial you will ever see. As I made my case against O.J., I was continually interrupted by cheering and thunderous applause. When the poor man came to the microphone to argue for the defense, he was booed before he even opened his mouth. I was sure I'd get a guilty verdict from the twelve people who had agreed to be jurors, but I hadn't reckoned on how many trips the bar servers were making to the jury box. When the trial ended, instead of leaving to deliberate, the jurors were told to stand up and announce their guilty or not-guilty votes. But by this time, one man was so drunk he *couldn't* stand up. The jurors on each side of him tried to pull him up by his arms, but he kept sliding out of their grasp and falling back into his chair. By this time, I had eleven guilty votes, but slapping and shaking couldn't revive this man, and we had to conclude with a hung jury—or as our Judge Ito put it, "a hungover jury."

The ship pulled into San Pedro early the next morning. And just like Clark Kent, I stepped back out of the phone booth and returned to my real life.

4. *Growing Up (a Little)*

After two years of college, I was tired of it. The only interesting part to me was the time spent on my social life. So when I came home for summer vacation, I decided to find a good job and wait until the end of summer to break it to my folks that I was not going back to school. I would tell them I was wasting my time and their money and that I would be better off to find a job and settle down. As you can see, I was very spoiled, unappreciative, and immature.

There were not many job openings for someone with my zero experience except in the food industry. But I finally found an opening at the San Francisco branch of the telephone company. I was hired to work in the billing department, which was way up on the nineteenth floor. Why I thought this would be more interesting than school, I can't imagine. My job was to sit and open endless remittance envelopes and enter the payments. As you can see, this was before the computer age, but then, so was I.

One day, instead of a check, I pulled out a letter and read the saddest story about why this woman couldn't pay her bill. I felt so sorry for her I got my checkbook out of my purse and made out a check to send to her. As I was writing a note to go with it, my curious supervisor leaned over my shoulder to see what I was doing. She laughed so loudly the whole office looked over. She ran around telling everyone that I was sending a check to one of their deadbeat accounts, and soon, the whole room was in an uproar.

I guess they decided I didn't have the right attitude for billing, so I was switched to a classroom where they were training girls to become service representatives. If you thought the old-time operators all sounded alike, it's because they were trained that way. Our training was to pick up our phones, and the teacher would start with a complaint. We were scripted to say exact phrases, such as, "Oh, I'm so sorry to hear that," or "Let me see how I can help you," etc. The class was boring but turned out to be very worthwhile, as it was where I met Kate and Jeanne, two other trainees. We became instant friends, and soon we three were staying after work to have dinner or to go out on the town. Kate lived in a nice duplex, but only because her folks owned the property and she could live there for free. So many nights, I stayed over with her rather than make a late-night ride across the bridge to my home in Berkeley.

The other tenants in the duplex were a family named Brubeck. It was the musician Dave Brubeck; his wife, Ollie; and two little boys. Dave and his group were just starting their careers, and they played in a club downtown. Many nights, we would drop in, and we felt like big shots when Dave would wave at us from the stage. No doubt he was especially nice to us because Kate was the landlord's daughter. When people buy his CDs now, I like to tell them that I was watching him perform back when he was making $100 a week and splitting it with his group.

When we graduated from class, we were given desks where

we received real complaints. During my first morning, a man came on my line who was so offensive and so obscene that at first, I couldn't believe my ears. I said nothing. I just froze, and then I threw the phone down on my desk as though it were covered with maggots. The supervisor had seen the expression on my face, I guess, and had already started to come over to my desk. She grabbed my phone and took over. She said he was a frequent caller and if he ever came in on any of our lines, to signal her and she would take care of him.

But all calls weren't bad. Kate had a very husky, sexy voice, and one man who called in completely forgot about his complaint when he heard her. He kept calling every day trying to get her to meet him after work, and she refused. Then one day, a deliveryman arrived at our floor and said he had a package addressed to "the girl with the sexy voice." He was led right to Kate's desk. The package contained a case of scotch. She never did agree to meet him, and the gift was a total waste on his part, as she didn't drink.

There was a lot of non-telephone activity going on every day. There were always people in the lunchroom cooking up snacks. And it seemed as though several times a week, someone had a birthday, so they'd phone downstairs to the St. Francis Bakery and have a rum cake sent up. There were also salespeople from various cosmetic companies allowed to roam around and let the girls try on creams and lotions. The restroom was aptly named, as at any time of the day, I could find at least one person stretched out on the couch taking a nap. This was allowed because the supervisors were as guilty as the rest of us. The work product from this floor must have been very low, but because these women had worked there for many years, management probably thought this was normal production.

My work as a service representative became easy, but not really interesting. I looked forward every day to quitting time, when Kate, Jeanne, and I would head out for an evening of fun. Every penny we made we spent on entertaining ourselves. One night, the three of us went to the House of Blue Lights and saw a brand-new singing sensation named Frankie Laine. When he sang his signature song, "That's My Desire," we three silly teenagers shrieked with joy, and he instantly stopped the music, came over to our table, and said, "Take it easy, girls!" while the audience roared. We heard later that he pulled that every night with some group of young girls who had been deliberately given a table at ringside. But it was still exciting to us at the time.

We were in the audience watching Gene Krupa's orchestra the night he was arrested on a drug charge. There's no doubt about it: San Francisco was a fun place to be if you were young and single.

But the fun was about to unravel. As September approached, Kate's parents were coaxing her to move back to her hometown of San Jose and start working in their family restaurant. Jeanne was also beginning to bow out of our nights out to spend time with a new boy she had met.

My parents were expecting me to pack up and return to school. It was time to tell them that I was going to continue on with my job. But a funny thing happened: I started to grow up a little. It was during the long train rides across the bridge that I started to sort things out. I was having a great time, but not during working hours. My job was boring, and what was kind of scary to me was that there were a lot of middle-aged people in my office doing things just as boring and they had been there for years. Did I really want to get stuck in oblivion at this point in my life? I could change jobs, but with no job qualifications, would I get anything better? Maybe I should stay in school, if for nothing else to sort of run in place while I decided what to do with myself.

Through the years since then, I have made some very good decisions and some not-so-good ones. But I have never regretted deciding not to spend my working years sitting on the nineteenth floor of the telephone company.

5. *What's in a Name?*

I have gone through many transitions regarding my name. When I started school, I didn't like it because no one could pronounce it. Vivian is not a difficult name for an adult, but children have trouble with the letter *v*. It usually comes out as a *b*. So I was called "Bibian." I probably couldn't pronounce it too well myself, but in my head, I heard it correctly.

When I went into the second grade with a new teacher, I thought I saw a solution to my problem. I would change my name to something easier to say. On the first day of school, the teacher asked each of us to stand up, greet the class, and introduce ourselves. When it was my turn, I stood up and said, "Good morning. My name is Mrs. Hamilton."

To her credit, the teacher didn't laugh. She just said, "Well, while you're in class, Mrs. Hamilton, I think I'll just call you Vivian."

As I grew older, I noticed that many of the girls in my class were named either Shirley or Barbara. There were so many that the teacher always had to say their entire names to differentiate. I didn't like this and thought what a nuisance it would be to sit with a whole row of Vivians. From then on, I liked having a fairly uncommon name.

At times, a name that is perfectly acceptable can become an embarrassment through no fault of your own. My daughter has a friend who learned to regret naming their son Charles. Their last name is Manson. They began calling him by his middle name.

Actually, it is fairly easy to legally change one's name. I think there will be a lot of name-changing going on when this current crop of Hollywood babies becomes old enough to see what awful names their parents have given them. How could Gwyneth Paltrow name her daughter "Apple"? And how could Julia Roberts name her son "Phinneas"?

My personal favorite is a Korean gentleman who sold real estate in Glendale about thirty years ago. I met him at an open house. He was quite handsome and well dressed, and he gravely handed me his business card as we talked. I glanced down at his name. His first name was spelled Y-U. His last name was Suk. There was no other way to pronounce it but "You suck." I kind of choked on the tea I had just been swallowing. Over his shoulder, I could see some friends of mine. They had been watching me to see my reaction when I read his card, and they were doubled up in laughter. I wonder if sometime in the following years, he changed it, but who knows? He is in sales, and it would certainly make an unforgettable impression on a prospect.

I would advise any young person who has an unusual name to try to work with it. But if you really hate it, just change it. Even after all these years, I know that if I should become involved in a front-page scandal, no problem. I'll just go back to telling people my name is Mrs. Hamilton.

6. *My Dream Man*

He put his arms around me, and I didn't resist. Instead, I found myself pulling closer to his insistent body. Then I awoke and realized that my exciting encounter had been a dream. I suppose many people have at one time or another had a sexual episode in a dream with some shadowy lover. But the man in this dream was not a stranger. It was Mr. Wilkins, a man who worked in my office. And he was a very ordinary man at that!

I had only been married for a few months. My husband was going to graduate school, and I had taken a job at a local credit bureau to support us. As I drove to work that morning, I thought about my strange dream. What had made Mr. Wilkins so attractive to my subconscious? I had to pass his desk on my way through the office, and I turned to take a better look at him. He looked up and smiled, and to my horror, I felt myself blushing.

"Good morning," he said, just like he said every morning.

I tried to give a casual greeting, but I stammered like an idiot. I dropped my purse, and I bumped into a chair when I bent to pick it up. Mr. Wilkins looked puzzled, and I didn't blame him.

I may have forgotten this whole bizarre episode if I hadn't had another dream about Mr. Wilkins. If anything, this one was even more erotic. When I awoke, my husband was lying there looking at me.

He knows! I thought in a panic.

"Must have been some dream." He laughed. "You were moaning and thrashing around. What was going on?"

"How would I know?" I lied. "I never remember a thing when I wake up."

I knew a woman named Marian who gave classes in dream interpretation. We'd remained friends after I took one of her classes, so I called and made a lunch date with her. It was time I found out what was going on inside my head. Of course, she laughed when I told her.

"Don't you remember from your classes that people are not always who they seem to be in your dreams? This man may look like someone you know, but it's possible he just represents some longing of yours. Is there some area of your life where you don't feel fulfilled?"

"Come on, Marian," I said. "That baloney's all right for your class, but don't think it'll work on me. I am having wild, vivid sex dreams, and my partner is a middle-aged nobody in my office that I've never even had a long conversation with. Nor ever wanted to. Is there any way you can help me?"

"What do you want me to do? It's *your* dream."

"Well, is there any way I can get him out of my head?"

Marian swirled the ice around in her glass and said, "You know, this is kind of interesting. Of course, I can't plot your dreams for you, you know that. But I'm a great believer that when we sleep, our brain continues to work on whatever problems we have been wrestling with. That is why so many times, one can go to sleep with an unsolved problem and wake up to figure out the answer. Well, I can't get this man out of your dream, but maybe we can do something to make him less attractive to you."

"He couldn't be any less attractive to me than he is right now!"

"Yes, but that's in your conscious life. Now, tonight, I want you to start thinking about all the things about him that are unappealing. And concentrate on these things just before you drift off to sleep. If it works, then maybe your sleeping mind won't be so darned friendly with him."

I couldn't do much about his personality because I didn't really know him. So I had to work solely on his appearance. When I went back to the office, I turned my desk chair so that I had a clear view of Mr. Wilkins, and I spent much of the afternoon trying to stare at him without being obvious.

His shiny, bald head was the first thing I noticed. This was not unattractive in itself, but it was definitely not the kind of head you would find on the cover of a Harlequin romance novel. So that was the first thing I wrote on my list. Then I remembered his ears! When I saw him that morning, before he even looked up, the first thing I noticed was all of the hairs sticking out. So I wrote down "hairy ears" on my list.

He got up to walk over to a filing cabinet. He had taken his jacket off, and I could see a little roll of fat hanging over his belt. Good. I added that to my list, but I had to laugh as I wrote this one down. My husband was in peak condition. And as a twenty-two-year-old, he still had lots of hair, and it was on his head, not coming out of his ears. What idiotic part of my brain was making me prefer Mr. Wilkins at night?

Before long, I had quite a list of things to contemplate as I waited to drop off to sleep. And each morning, I was careful to follow Marian's instructions on dream recollection: don't open your eyes, and don't speak—the least little distraction and the dream will be gone from your memory.

Night after night, the few dream fragments I could remember had nothing to do with Mr. Wilkins. Marian called me about a week later, and I told her I wasn't having any luck. She said the fact that I was not dreaming about him at all could be because I had made him so unappealing, but I am not sure that she or I had anything to do with it. I think this freak occurrence just ran its course and ended as mysteriously as it began.

I'm a senior citizen now, so that happened many decades ago. I look back at it now with great amusement. And I can't help but wonder: "Where are you, Mr. Wilkins, now that I'm alone?"

7. The Book Club

When my third child was born, my first child was less than three years old, so I led quite a busy life in those days. I loved my babies, but the only books I had around the house were in rhymes and had pop-up pictures. I began to wonder if my brain was going to atrophy.

One day, I was reading a magazine in the pediatrician's office, and there was a full-page ad displaying four books, all of them on the best-seller list and all of them ones I wanted to read. In large letters, it said, "Only $4.98!" Maybe this would give me a little mental stimulation. I tore the page out, and when I got home, I signed it and sent it in with my check. When I told my husband, Gregg, that I was getting four best-sellers for $4.98, he thought it a terrific deal and said that it would give me something to do.

Something to do? I hadn't thought about that. I already had *plenty* to do. Just when would I be able to read them? A week later, there was a box on my front porch containing my new books. I

25

put them up on the mantelpiece, out of the reach of little hands. But as much as I tried, I could never get all three children to take naps at the same time. There was always one of them I had to keep an eye on, and that is no way to enjoy a book.

A month went by, and when the mailman arrived, he left a familiar-looking box on the front porch. In it were four more books and a bill for $4.98. *This must be a mistake,* I thought. I went through my desk and found the top of the book order. I hadn't just ordered four books; I had joined a book club, promising to buy four new books a month for one year. At this point, I hadn't even had time to open the first book yet. I should have contacted the company right then and found out what the penalty was for dropping out. In fact, I never should have opened the second box, because these new books were all books that everyone was talking about and I *did* want to read them. I put them on top of the piano and hoped Gregg wouldn't notice.

Fortunately, I did the bill paying in our family. It was not as though $4.98 a month would push us into bankruptcy. It was just that I didn't want to admit to him that I had been so stupid that I'd signed a contract without reading it.

That month, I truly tried to get some reading done. Daytime was impossible, but at night, after dinner when the children were in bed for the night, I would curl up on the couch and begin reading. But every time I did that, I was sound asleep in minutes.

Another month went by, and another box was left on my front porch. I took the books out and looked around with a slight feeling of panic. So far, he hadn't even noticed the books on the piano, but even an unobservant husband like Gregg was bound to notice a lot of new books sooner or later. I walked around the house looking for a hiding place and cleared a space behind the towels in the linen closet. This lasted for the next two deliveries, and then I ran out of space again.

I took book number one with me everywhere I went,

hoping for a chance to finish it. But every time I had a few minutes, I forgot what had happened and had to go back to a previous chapter to refresh my memory.

I began to dread the first of the month, because I knew I would see another box on my porch. I put these books under my bed, and there was so much space there, I put the next four books under there too. One night, I had a dream that we moved to another town, and when we dismantled our bed, this huge mountain of books fell on us.

One day, my three-year-old cried out, "Book, Mommy! Book!" and came into the room clutching one of my hidden books. While I had been changing the baby, she had dragged a footstool over to the linen closet to explore. Behind the towels, she had discovered my stash of books.

I guess that did it. I could lead this double life no longer. I called the book company and asked for the manager. I identified myself and said I had ordered these books for my mother and they had been a great deal of comfort to her in her last days.

"But," I said in a tremulous voice, "she died this week, so I have no more use for them."

"I am *so* sorry!" he exclaimed, sounding like he really meant it.

"Thank you," I said bravely. "Do you suppose … Is there any way … Could I possibly cancel her contract?"

"Of course. I'll have the paperwork put through immediately. I am just happy that your mother had such pleasure from her membership while she could."

The books stopped arriving, and the nightmare was over. Gregg built a bookshelf to show off his golf trophies, and I quietly and gradually brought my books out of hiding and put them on one of the shelves. Gregg noticed them and even commented on some of the titles he recognized. But he never questioned how I managed to purchase twenty-eight books for $4.98.

8. *The Intruder*

When I recognized the droppings on the sink counter, I knew that somewhere there was a mouse in my house. What I didn't know was what battle of wits lay ahead of me.

I went to the hardware store to buy a trap, and I guess the salesman could see how skittish I was. The huge snapping sound when he set one of the traps off was a little intimidating. So he sold me what they probably sell only to scared old ladies: a rectangle of really sticky stuff with what looks like a little food in the center. *Very clever,* I thought. *When the little devil walks over to eat, he gets stuck.* It wasn't until I put it on my sink that it occurred to me that it wouldn't kill him. Instead, I might wake up to a very angry mouse trying desperately to pull his foot out.

I heard a noise that night and found the trap on the

kitchen floor. There was no mouse in it, but it did have a very good set of prints in case I wanted to get the FBI involved. I put the sticky trap back on the sink, but the mouse never went near it again.

This made me think of when I was in school and we learned about one way that mice were tested in mazes. As I recall, if the mouse turned left, he got a small electrical jolt. If he turned right, he got food. In no time at all, the mouse would just turn right. So even though my intruder had a tiny brain, he had a darned good memory. It was time for a new approach.

I went back to the hardware store and bought one of those lethal-looking wooden traps. I also bought a jar of peanut butter, as the salesman said it was really popular with mice. I wasn't all that interested in pleasing the mouse's palate, but I wanted to get this over with fast.

There was no sign of him the next morning. Could he have been watching from some hiding place while I set it? I knew he had a memory that was probably better than mine, but how many cells could there be in his brain?

The following night, he returned and prowled around my kitchen. There was no mystery about where he roamed. Just as Hansel and Gretel dropped bread crumbs, he left a trail of droppings—not as aesthetically pleasing, but just as effective. At first, he just ran around on the sink, but I don't know what pleasure he gained from this, as there was no food left out. Because of him, I put my fruit bowl in the refrigerator and even began a daily shaking of my toaster over the sink in case he had a taste for bread crumbs.

The next morning, I found droppings on my stove top. My new trap sat there on the sink with that delicious glob of peanut butter, and he paid no attention. What could attract him to the stove? There was no spilled food, just a clean enamel surface. I gingerly picked up the loaded trap on the sink and moved it to the stove. It sat there, undisturbed, for three days, which was very inconvenient; I was not about to cook next to a mousetrap, so each day, I would gingerly move it back to the sink.

The third morning, I came in and saw that the peanut butter was gone. But there was no mouse. He'd carefully licked it all off without springing the trap! How could he do this? I could see that I would have to be careful not to underestimate my opponent. He'd obviously been around mousetraps a lot longer than I had.

This was the day that he made a sort of statement. Instead of random droppings, there were a few at each corner of the trap. Did he leave them there as he slowly walked around the trap planning his strategy? Was I getting paranoid, or was he giving me the "finger" in his own mouse language?

Hoping to confuse him at least as much as he was confusing me, that night, I re-peanut-buttered the trap, put it back on the stove, and wedged the sticky trap next to it, hoping he'd get stuck in one while he tried to avoid the other. He retaliated by expertly picking off the peanut butter and then flipping the other trap facedown on one of the burners. It took two days to soak the goop off of that burner.

I wonder if Dr. Seuss ever wrote a book called *A Mouse in the House*? If so, I'll bet his mouse was cute and spoke in rhymes. But my mouse was not cute. I finally saw him one night when I went into the kitchen. When I turned on the light, to my horror, this little creature with a long tail raced across the floor from the stove to the dishwasher, disappearing into the corner. And I mean he totally vanished. I knelt down and peered at the corner. I'd had my dishwasher replaced, and the new one was about a half inch narrower than the opening. I put a small can of soup on its side, and it seemed to block the hole—I thought. But that night, he managed to get past the can and let me know it all over my stove. I was finding that a mouse could somehow squeeze his body through unbelievably tiny spaces.

I started to get into the spirit of this battle of wits we were having. I bought a crazy-looking trap that consisted of a piece of cardboard completely sticky on one side. It folded into a tent with an opening on each end. According to the directions, when he walked in, the inside would stick to every part of him. He might be able to walk around with this tent stuck to him, but surely he couldn't fit through a small hole to make his getaway. I set it next to the soup can, confident that in all his experience, he'd never come across a Trojan tent before.

He didn't fall for the tent, but he got in anyway. I know because I saw him again the next night, just as he walked over and disappeared behind the soup can. He wasn't even running. Apparently, he had such contempt for me by then that he just sort of sauntered along.

This was no longer fun. I was beginning to get mad. This creature that was outwitting me was almost the bottom of the food chain. I went back to the hardware store and bought four more traps, set them, and placed them all around the kitchen. I hoped I'd remember not to step into them.

The next morning brought an alarming new development. I don't know if it was the heavy display of traps, but for the first time, my intruder had left the kitchen. I found droppings on the lamp table next to the living room chair that I sat in when I was watching television. And just for the tiniest second, I found myself wondering if while I was in bed at night, he was sitting in my chair trying to work the remote. What was happening to me? Was I now beginning to slide into madness?

The next morning, I started down the hallway to the kitchen and stopped. On the threshold between the kitchen and hall was an overturned trap with a long tail sticking out. I was so surprised I just stood there for a moment, my brain trying to compute what my eyes were seeing. Then I gingerly picked up the trap and deposited it into a paper bag, which I folded up and took directly out to the trash barrel. I never turned it over; I didn't want to see his face. The trap was at least a foot away from where I had placed it in the kitchen, and I didn't like the idea that maybe his death had not been instantaneous. Did he maybe have a James Cagney–like death where he kept getting back on his feet?

I had won. But why didn't I feel more elated? I guess because I couldn't help admiring my opponent. He'd been able to recognize and circumvent each new trap I set for him. I was a human being with a college education. He was a tiny creature with nothing but his native wits and his incredible memory to use against me. And actually, he didn't take up space and ate nothing of mine but the peanut butter.

I've had houseguests who were a lot more trouble than that.

9. *The New Board Game*

Those of you who were not born into the high-tech age may miss the board games of old. We could understand them, for one thing. And they were simple enough that we didn't have to go back to school to play. This is a pitch from a company who is trying to create a market in the vast, untapped senior generation.

"Ladies and Gentlemen, I am a representative from the ACME Game Company, and I have a new board game that I'm sure you will want to order before the Christmas rush. I think you will agree that the biggest game sellers today are electronic and they concentrate on violence and sex. These have made board games seem very tame in comparison, and sales have been slow. *Our* new board game will bring all that excitement back to the players.

"It is a game for senior citizens called 'Driving Thru Town.' It is set up for four players. Starting at the same time, each will cross his hometown, trying to be the first to reach the pharmacy to fill his prescription.

"To demonstrate the exciting possibilities of this game, I have asked four volunteers to play it for you. I'll call them players A, B, C, and D. Each player will now draw a game piece. Player A has a 1979 Buick. Player B has a motorized sidewalk scooter. Player C has a bus, and Player D has a taxi. Let the games begin.

"Player A guns his Buick and draws a card. Too bad, Player A, the card says, 'They are filling potholes on your block this morning. You cannot get your car out of the driveway.'

"Player B puts his cane across the back of his scooter and draws a card. It says, 'Proceed two blocks. Panhandler steps in front of you. Contribute $10, or he will take your scooter away from you.'

"Player C boards the bus and draws a card. It says, 'Bus was late, but it makes up for it by sailing past the next two stops, leaving the people still sitting on the benches.' Good luck, Player C, you are off to a speedy start.

"Player D gets in his waiting taxi and draws a card. What's this? 'The cab driver doesn't speak English.' How can he tell him to rush to the pharmacy? He shows his prescription to the driver who shrugs and lights a large cigar.

"It is Player A's turn again. His next card tells him that he can go around the potholes by driving on the sidewalk, and he has now reached Main Street. There is gridlock. He only moves one block on this turn.

"Player B draws the 'Go to Jail' card. Too bad. He would have been better off to pay that panhandler the $10 instead of hitting him with his cane.

"Player C is having trouble staying on his seat; the bus is going so fast. This is good, he thinks, as he draws a card. But no. This is not good. The card says his bus is going in the wrong direction.

"Player D is now using sign language in a desperate effort

to communicate with the cab driver. He draws a card that says, 'The driver points straight ahead,' and D happily cries, 'Yes!' The cab moves forward.

"This is where the game gets exciting. Who will win the race? Will it be A, who is in the midst of gridlock? B, who is trying to arrange bail? C, who is barreling along on a bus going in the wrong direction? Or D, whose only communication thus far has been to point at his windshield?

"I am sure you see the potential for our new game. Soon, it will be a part of the Saturday-night festivities in retirement homes all over. Let the young folks have their games where they try to blow each other up. The old folks will experience all the action and excitement they need, just trying to cross their own hometown."

10. *Papa's Earthquake*

The year was 2050. I walked up the stairs of the newly opened high-tech history museum and paid my entry fee. An attendant led me to a small room containing a large flat-screen on the wall, plus a comfortable-looking lounge chair with a keyboard on a small table beside it. The attendant left, closing the door behind her.

I typed in "Edward Wilbur Parker," and then I typed "April 18, 1906." Since I was paying by the hour, I had decided to begin that day at 4:30 am.

I pressed "Enter" and settled back. At first, the screen seemed to be black, and then I saw that it was clouded with dark swirls of fog. I could make out the running lights of a boat. Three young men were standing at the railing drinking coffee and laughing. One of them, the one the camera seemed to be closing in on, was a good-looking lad. He was short, very cute, and had a big grin on his face. He was bundled up, as were the others, and some of his blond locks had escaped from his watch cap and were blowing in the wind. One of his friends called him "Eddie." I leaned forward. Could this laughing young man be my great-grandfather? The dignified old man that everyone had called "Papa"?

In the background, I could see the ferry building and the huge clock that said 4:30. He must be on the ferryboat making his early morning commute across the bay to his job at the *San Francisco Chronicle*. The ferry pulled into the landing, but before it closed the gap, while it was still being tied down, he and his lively companions had already jumped onto the shore. For a moment, I wanted to call out to him to go back, stay on the boat, take it back across the bay. In just one hour, I wanted to tell him, there will be a major earthquake that will set off the largest fire in the history of this country. But then, I realized how ridiculous I was being. I couldn't change history. And besides, Papa lived to be an old man. So I already knew that he would be all right.

This lad, Eddie, had left his friends and was now at his desk in the *Chronicle* building. I would have liked to see him busily typing away, working on a big story, but actually, he seemed to be taking advantage of the fact that few people had come to work yet. He was leaning way back in his chair with his feet on his desk, wadding pieces of scratch paper and trying to toss them into a nearby wastepaper basket. The cleaning woman came in, and she threw a few shots into the basket. They were talking and laughing. *Come on, Papa, I was thinking, the future is watching you. Do something important.*

And then I saw it. A slight tremor caused a pencil on his desk to roll, and then came the first ominous creaking sound. This accelerated rapidly into a deafening roar. Eddie's chair fell over backward throwing him to the floor just as a huge ceiling fixture crashed down upon his desk. A large filing cabinet toppled over, trapping the cleaning woman, and I heard her muffled scream. Eddie crawled over and tried to push the cabinet aside, but it was too late. Her head had been crushed, and he looked at it with a dazed expression. Things were happening so fast I didn't know where to look. The wall beside Eddie collapsed, and just like that, he was outside the building.

Eddie's two friends somehow found him through all the pandemonium. Instead of running to find a safe spot away from the buildings, they began their own search-and-rescue operation. People were beginning to stagger out of their apartments and offices. I could see an office building across the street; one entire brick wall had fallen, exposing six stories of rooms with people staring out in disbelief. As the camera followed Eddie and his friends, I saw more and more people out on the sidewalk, confused and scared. One woman was clutching a flatiron, as though somehow in her terrified mind, she had considered this to be important to save.

Electric wires were down, and gas lines had ruptured. Small fires were starting everywhere I could see. History books have told me that it would be three days before the fire department could put these fires out, and by that time, two hundred thousand people would be homeless. But Eddie and his friends didn't know what an uphill fight they were waging, as they foraged through the wreckage pulling people out of dangerously leaning structures. At one point, Eddie stopped and ran down an alley in search of a mewing sound he somehow heard over all the commotion. He picked up a little white kitten and stuffed it into his jacket pocket. I saw its head peering out at all the screams and sirens in the streets.

It was now early evening. They had been working nonstop to help people all day. I saw them walk into a building and come out with arms full of blankets and pillows. They were heading for a park to get some rest. Behind them, the view of San Francisco was heartbreaking: no tall buildings, no skyline at all, few people moving around anymore, and fires in every direction. The earthquake lasted less than one minute, but that is an eternity with a major shake. The park they picked was filling up with desperate-looking people who had nowhere to go.

I had seen enough. I pushed the stop button and went out to pay the balance of my bill. It was expensive but worth every penny. I walked back down the stairs with a whole new feeling about my great-grandfather. I knew him mainly from pictures and loving stories from my mother, and my mental picture was of a wrinkled, bald, and rather formal old man. Now I could see that he was brave, caring, and funny. And the most fun of all was to find out that Papa was a hunk!

11. *Medical Breakthroughs in the Next Century?*

Past generations would be astounded that man has progressed to the point of actually being able to repair or replace so many vital parts of our bodies. The first transplants were performed in life-or-death situations. Then, in the next stage, many were performed just for vanity. Who knows what will be in effect by the end of this century? Perhaps by the year 2100, if you need a body part, you will just be able to drive to the nearest distributor. It will probably be called "Parts R Us," and you will be able to stroll up and down the refrigerated aisles looking for a match.

Cremations will become rarer as people will have a financial reason to want to keep their bodies intact. If they do not have much of an estate to leave, they can bequeath their parts on consignment to Parts R Us. When one is purchased, the payment will go into the estate of the deceased, minus the cost of the refrigeration and shipping.

Perhaps we will get catalogs through the mail showing non-vital parts that are negotiable. You could flip through the pages looking for something that appealed to you. These parts would still be on the donors so the price would have to be fairly steep in order to persuade the donor to part with whatever you wanted. But there might be a surprising number of people who would part with a foot, say, in exchange for enough money to see them through their senior years.

Surely, it wouldn't be long before someone opened a website offering trades. Obviously, the worse you look, the harder it would be to make a trade, because when you got the new part, the donor would be stuck with the part that you didn't want. For instance, if you have a bulbous nose, you would have a problem trading it for someone's normal-sized nose, so you would have to sweeten the pot, say, by throwing in your thick head of hair. You can always buy a toupee, but it's hard to hide a nose.

And there would no doubt be a large section of breasts. Many a well-endowed older woman might be very happy to trade her huge bosom for a smaller, more comfortable one.

This might actually be one answer to capital punishment. Some people are convicted of crimes so heinous that they don't deserve to go on living. But there will always be those who protest that it is wrong to take a life. Instead of spending twenty years on death row filing appeals, young, healthy convicts could be given the choice between death and switching body parts. A good-looking prisoner would no doubt cause quite a bidding war. A notice would be posted to all interested parties, and they would be given three days to look him over. Then the bidding would begin on eBay. He would have to assume the body parts of the highest bidders, which could leave this former Adonis with a bald head, sunken chest, flat nose, and potbelly, and even his long legs could be traded for short ones.

Full-length mirrors would face the cells of these convicts so that every morning, they could see how they looked and contemplate the crimes that had led them to this fate. This would not only be a fitting revenge, it could create a highly entertaining reality show for television.

There is just one thing this future generation will have to be careful about: they must make sure that each contract is signed by the person directly involved. Otherwise, the first time a husband manages to transplant his entire wife, part by part, the lawsuits will begin.

12. *3 Things I Wouldn't Do For Money*

It was late at night, and a few of us were sitting by the fire finishing up the wine. We were talking about money, and my friend Carl was insisting that for the right price, you could get anyone to do anything. I didn't like to think that was true, but I couldn't think of anything to refute this. And neither could anyone else.

The next day, I kept thinking about his cynical belief. Surely there were actions I wouldn't take, even in the face of an astronomical fortune. And then, I thought of one: I would not smoke. No, no matter what the prize. As a teenager, I began smoking. I remember the first cigarette didn't taste good; in fact, it made me dizzy. But I forced myself to continue because all my friends smoked. And why did we all smoke? Because we wanted to look cool like the movie stars. In no time at all,

43

I was a chain-smoker. I would literally light my new cigarette from my old one.

One day after I married, my mother-in-law took me with her to visit her best friend who had just moved into a beautiful new home. We sat in the living room while her friend went into the kitchen to bring us some coffee. Without thinking about it, I pulled out a cigarette and lit it. My mother-in-law was frantic. She said her friend didn't allow smoking in her home. She said to get rid of it, but where? Obviously, there were no ashtrays. I sprinted across the room to throw it out a window, but I couldn't open the screen. In desperation, I stuck it into the water of a bud vase to put it out and then put the soggy thing in my pocket. By this time, I really wanted to quit but couldn't seem to do so. I would decide the minute the pack was empty, that was it. But then, I would just buy another one. I read an article that said you have to become the boss of yourself to quit a habit such as smoking. Carry an open pack around with you, and tell yourself you can smoke if you want to, you just don't want to. Could it really be as simple as that? I put an open pack in my pocket and just from habit would reach for it. Then I would say to myself, "No, I don't think I will."

By some miracle I still don't understand, I never smoked again. And I thought of Carl's statement the night before. I am sure that he could offer me an absolute fortune, and I would not light a cigarette. Because if I did, the same addictive personality that I saw before would make me keep on, and by tomorrow, I would be chain-smoking again.

And then I thought about something else I wouldn't do. I thought about the countless women I have either known or read about who willingly married men they didn't love, simply because the man had great wealth. And I decided I'd add this to my list. No matter how much money was involved, I would not marry a man if his wealth was absolutely all he had to offer.

My theory is that if you marry for money, you end up earning every penny of it.

I had a friend named Betty who worked for a man who was incredibly wealthy. Everyone in town knew this. He owned a large business and had made no secret of the fact that he was attracted to my friend. But the feeling was definitely not mutual. She told me many times that she found him boring and unattractive. So I was very surprised when she said he had proposed to her and she was thinking seriously about accepting. I said, "How could you even get in bed with him, let alone marry him?"

She just smiled and said, "No problem. I'll just lie there and think about my net worth."

So they married, and not even a year later, he had a stroke and could no longer run his business. Instead of spending her days shopping and spending, she suddenly became his nurse. If she had loved him, this would have been all right, but she didn't even like him, and she complained to me all the time.

But wait——it gets worse. The supposedly trustworthy man he put in charge of his business cheated him, and he ended up losing everything, including his home. I felt as though I were watching a morality play.

I couldn't wait to talk to Carl. I had thought of not only one but two things that no amount of money would make me do.

And then I thought of another, the most important one of all. I would never, never let anyone confine me in a small covered space that I could not get out of by myself. The granddaddy of all fears of this type would be to be buried alive.

During Victorian times, this was a widespread fear. Medical technology was not very advanced, and probably this happened more times than we like to think. So they started the practice of burying the corpse with a string tied around his finger. This string ran up above the ground where it was attached to a bell. If the body should revive, it could wiggle its finger, and the bell would ring. This is where we got the expression "Saved by the bell."

Well, of course, in spite of my fears, I would never do something as silly as that. I shall simply leave a request that I be buried with my cell phone—just in case.

13. *The $2,800 Diet*

I had joined the sales staff of a large company.
Our Friday morning meetings always included coffee and
doughnuts. On many weekends, there were promotional
cocktail parties. Slowly and insidiously, the weight crept on.
Ten pounds might not sound like much, but if you are short, it
can be the difference of a whole dress size, and I was running
out of clothes to wear.
I decided to end this destructive cycle before it got worse. I had
a week's vacation coming up, so I phoned a famous reducing
spa and made a reservation. It was expensive, but I wanted
quick results. I spent a grueling week being bullied, prodded,
and pushed through hikes and exercises that lasted most of the
day. My stomach was in such pain I could hardly bend it to sit
up in the morning and just sort of rolled out of bed.
   During this ordeal, I was fed what seemed to be the barest
minimum of calories a day. At the end of the week, my weight

loss was 4 1/2 pounds. I was stunned. It seemed to me I should have lost that much the first day. This miserable week cost me $2,000! I had paid over $400 per pound!

I had never tried to lose weight before and somehow thought it would be easier. Then, to my consternation, as my work and social life continued, those 4 1/2 pounds climbed right back on. I spent a long time feeling sorry for myself. Then I heard about a relatively inexpensive fat farm not too far from my town, and I made a reservation.

Einstein once said, "Insanity is doing the same thing over and over and expecting the result to be different." I should have listened to him.

This spa was $50 a day, which seemed like peanuts compared to what I had paid before. When I got there, I saw why: no comfort, no service, and above all, no privacy. I was given a room with two strangers. I had trouble sleeping because of their nonstop talking and giggling. I shivered because they wanted the air-conditioning on all night. This spa had a gymnasium, but there were no supervised programs, so many of the guests sat by the pool all day playing cards and waiting for the next meal. I couldn't figure why they were there unless it was a chance to get away from their families.

At mealtime, we were given our choice of two hundred, four hundred, or nine hundred calories per day. Since I wasn't there to play bridge, I grimly picked the two hundred. You should see two hundred calories split into three meals. I wouldn't be surprised if the fresh flowers on my table contained more nourishment than what was on my plate.

The result of this week was a five-pound loss—$70 per pound! And weren't these the same pounds I'd paid to lose before?

Two months after my return from the second spa, those pounds were back and so was my depression. What good did it do to lose weight if it was temporary? I had to learn how to <u>keep</u> the pounds off.

Would you believe I got out my checkbook once again? This time, I paid $495 to a behavior modification clinic for a three-month course. I was told to buy a calorie book and a food scale. Then I was given a calorie limit and told I could eat anything I wanted every day up to my limit. The book was quite a revelation. The cocktails and hors d'oeuvres I consumed at just one party exceeded my entire day's calorie limit. No wonder the pounds were accumulating!

Every Saturday, I had to bring something in to the clinic for breakfast and sit and eat it in front of an instructor. For convenience, I stopped at a McDonald's each week and bought an Egg McMuffin. I had to eat this with a knife and fork, putting the utensils down between each bite, and I had to spend fifteen minutes finishing this meal. This is a long time. Their point was that if you bolt your food down, you keep eating while your brain is trying to tell you that you are full.

For once, my money was not wasted. At the end of the three months, my ten pounds were gone, and I could thankfully wear all of my clothes again. When I went into the office wearing a dress I hadn't been able to squeeze into for a long time, the receptionist glanced up at me and said, "Goodness but you're getting thin!"

I couldn't help but think of Mae West's famous line, "Goodness had nothing to do with it, Dearie."

14. Conversations with O.J., Osama, and Others

When I came home that cloudy October day, I noticed a strange cable truck at the curb. My company is Charter, but the lettering on the side of this truck read, "Veritas." There was no one in the truck. I looked up at the houses around me and could see no one working. But this was of no concern to me, and I forgot about it until later that night. My sister, Joanne, had gone to bed, and I was watching an old movie on TV, when a message crawled across the bottom of the screen that said, "Turn to Channel 780." I sat up and rubbed my eyes, but the message was coming back repeating itself.

I pressed the numbers to find a screen that was almost entirely taken up by a man's head. He didn't exactly look sinister, but he didn't look jovial either. He seemed to be looking directly at me as he said, "Welcome to my private channel. I am Mr. Veritas. For $1,000, I can offer you what no one else can. I can give you the chance to ask one question to three people of your choice, and they must tell the truth. If you want to enter into my world, press the zero on your remote."

What was this? Some crazy advertising gimmick? I'd had some wine with my dinner, but not enough that I would be hallucinating. I turned and called out, "Joanne! Come in here! Hurry!"

Joanne ran in, and I motioned to her to sit beside me on the couch. The screen had gone dark. I picked up the remote and pressed the zero. "Hello?" I said, feeling a little stupid.

The screen lit up, and once again, Mr. Veritas was staring out at me. "Finished thinking it over? Want to go ahead?"

For Joanne's benefit, I asked him to repeat his offer. Then I said, "Well, in the first place, I think $1,000 is awfully steep. Do you realize how many movies and specials I could watch for that?"

"Madam, how can you even compare them to what I am offering? Come! Come! I have other customers not as unappreciative as you."

I looked at Joanne, and she was starting to laugh. "It's some kind of joke," she whispered. "Go along with it."

"Well …" This was difficult. Even though I didn't believe him for a minute, I didn't want to waste my three picks.

"I know!" I said. "I've got a real challenge for you. This man doesn't know the meaning of the word *truth*. My first pick is O. J. Simpson. But I want my money's worth. When I ask my question, I want media coverage and I want his children and friends, if he has any, to be there when he answers. Is this possible?"

"Anything is possible."

There was a brief moment of snow and static, and then there was O.J. looking at the camera. He looked puzzled and, for him, very subdued. His children stood beside him, and I could see a local news truck parked nearby.

"Mr. Simpson," said Mr. Veritas, "it is time for you to tell the truth. Did you murder Ron and Nicole?"

There was a close-up of O.J.'s face. He stared into the camera for what seemed like a long moment and finally, quietly, said, "Yes."

And the snow and static returned, and I was back with Mr. Veritas.

"How did you do that? What's this all about?" I glanced at Joanne. She was no longer laughing.

"How I do this would be hard to explain to you. I'm not from your planet, and we have advanced far beyond the earth in technology. I'm here on a research grant studying *truth*. There is so little truth in your world anymore, and we believe that truth is vital for any planet to survive and prosper. While I'm here, I intend to straighten things out as much as I can.

"I'm sure you realize that Mr. Simpson has already been tried, so he can't be taken to court again. But I think I understand why you asked what you did. And by making him tell the truth to the world, it surely will bring some measure of satisfaction to a lot of people. Whom do you want to question next?"

Joanne grabbed my arm. "Jeffrey!" she whispered. "Find out what happened to Jeffrey!"

I turned back to the TV. "A boy named Jeffrey Holmquist stood me up on a date a long time ago. He never showed up and never even called with an explanation. I'm still angry. I want to hear the truth from him about that night."

Mr. Veritas looked at me disdainfully. "I had hoped for a little more important question from you."

"It's my thousand dollars," I said defensively. "And by the way, if you're from another planet, what good would our money be to you anyway?"

"None whatsoever. I just charge an amount high enough to weed out nuisance calls, which I hope this is not becoming. Do you really want to ask your second question?"

"Yes."

When the screen cleared, a man appeared who was a total stranger to my eyes. And he looked quite old. Where O.J. had looked forlorn, Jeffrey looked confused.

Mr. Veritas said, "You had a date to take a seventeen-year-old girl to a play, and you stood her up and never apologized or gave an excuse. To this day, she is angry."

"What's this all about?" he said crossly. "You've got me mixed up with someone else."

"I have the tickets right here, sir. Eighth row, Curran Theatre, San Francisco. The name of the play was *Charlie's Aunt*. Now do you remember?"

The look on Jeffrey's face was priceless, as one could almost watch the realization dawning upon him. "I remember now! That morning, my mother's sister was in a terrible car crash in Iowa, and she asked me to drive her back there. I just plain forgot about the play. I should have called her, but it's not like she was my girlfriend. In fact, that would have been our first date."

"And you didn't explain it to her even after you came back?"

"But I didn't come back. Mother stayed to help her sister, and I finished school in Iowa. I was just a dumb teenager. My God, and she's still mad?"

The screen dissolved into snow again. And then Mr. Veritas reappeared.

"You have just one question left, madam. I hope you won't waste it trying to put another bandage on your wounded ego."

I was all business now. "You bet I won't waste it. I've had a little time to think, and I've got a dilly for you. But you have to set it up. I want you to arrange for this third telecast to be seen by the officer in charge of our special forces in Iraq. Then I want you to talk to Osama bin Laden."

"And your question?"

"With the military watching, I want you to ask him exactly, and I mean precisely, where he is at this moment."

15. Kiwi

Our next-door neighbor Isabel was going to spend the summer in Europe. She asked if she could leave her parrot, Kiwi, with us, and we didn't see any problem with that. In fact, we were flattered, as she didn't seem too friendly with anyone else on the block.

I was going to put Kiwi's cage and stand on the back porch as I'd heard that birds could be messy, but Isabel wouldn't hear of it.

"She's very clean and has good manners. Keep her in the den, or she'll be lonesome."

At first, my husband and I laughed every time Kiwi said a distinguishable word. Mainly, she seemed to talk about herself, repeating phrases as, "Kiwi hungry," or "Kiwi nice little bird."

One day, Kiwi blurted out, "Isabel! Drinking again?" I stopped everything to listen, but that was the end of her communication for the day.

I couldn't wait for Carl to get home and greeted him with, "Today, Kiwi said someone was accusing Isabel of drinking!"

"What, that stuffy old lady? I can't believe she would take anything stronger than an occasional sip of sherry!"

Maybe Kiwi was listening to us, because she called out, "Awk! Margarita time!"

Isabel was the "proper" lady of the neighborhood and quick to gossip about anyone who wasn't. I must confess; we were enjoying this immensely.

During the summer, we spent much time with Kiwi, hearing terse comments from Isabel's phone conversations and much confidential information that we listened to and laughed at shamelessly. It wasn't until the end of August that we suddenly remembered that Kiwi was also listening to us.

One night, she said, "Just imagine! Isabel's a drunk! Just imagine!" and we froze. How could we return Kiwi in this condition? Isabel would know how we'd laughed at her all summer.

Carl said, "We can't get all our words out of that parrot's head; just forget it. We'll just have to hope she doesn't listen to Kiwi as closely as we do."

But I said, "Well, maybe I can teach her some kind of disclaimer." And all that last week, I kept saying three words to her over and over: "Kiwi just kidding! Kiwi just kidding!"

Isabel came home, and we returned the parrot. I don't know what Kiwi said about us, but Isabel never spoke to us again.

16. *Funny Money*

Laura walked into the restaurant and came over to my booth. As she sat down across from me, she slapped a twenty-dollar bill onto the table and said, "Guess what this is."

"Unless I'm blind, it's a twenty-dollar bill."

At this point, the waitress came over, dropped a couple of menus, and walked off.

"Miss, could you please bring some water?" Laura called, but she was gone.

"I already tried that. She moves pretty fast when she's leaving the table."

She pulled the money out from under the menus and said, "Do you remember my uncle Albert?"

"The one who went to prison for counterfeiting? How could I forget?"

"Well, he used to live at our house on and off. Anytime he

56

had a fight with Aunt Emma, my dad would let him sleep in our attic. He had a regular bedroom up there."

"I remember that. Didn't he die in prison?"

"Yes, a few years ago. So this week, I'm turning the attic into an office, and there was a little corner that was boarded up. Today, I opened it and found this paper bag full of money that Albert probably stashed in case he decided not to go back to Emma. That's why I called and asked you to meet me for lunch. I just had to confide in someone. I have five hundred of these bills right here in my purse! That's ten thousand dollars! Can you believe my good luck?"

"Why are you carrying all that around with you?"

"Right after lunch, it goes straight into my safety deposit box. I just wanted to show it to you first!"

The waitress appeared, and we ordered fast before we lost her again. "I'll have a petit filet, blood rare," I said. "And we still don't have any water."

Laura decided upon her entrée, and the minute we were alone, I said, "You don't have some crazy idea about trying to spend this money, do you?"

"Why not? The Feds don't even know about it."

"You don't know what they know. There might have been something about those bills that helped them catch Albert. Don't forget, they've changed the look of the twenty since he went to prison. If you suddenly flood the area with the old ones, someone might notice."

"I wouldn't flood the area, just a few bills here and there every week. I'll be careful."

"That's probably just what Albert said. If they catch you, they'll think you were in it with him. You'd end up in prison just like he did."

Suddenly, a large plate of greens was dumped in front of each of us, and we jumped back out of the way. I looked up at the waitress as she was turning to leave. "Hey!" I said. "There's no dressing on this."

She pulled out her pad. "Whatcha want?"

"Whatcha got?" I said, deliberately mimicking her.

She rattled off a list, and we made our selections. After she left, Laura said, "Why'd you pick this place? Because of the courteous service?"

"Never mind her; it's you I'm worried about. Sure, there's probably only about a 1 percent chance you'd get caught, but look at the moral side to this. Anytime you give a counterfeit bill to someone, you are cheating him out of the real money that he deserves, because maybe when he tries to spend it, he'll get caught. Doesn't that bother you?"

She patted her purse lovingly and said, "Not yet."

The salad dressing arrived, but at the same time as our entrées. I would have preferred to have my salad first, but then again, I would have preferred to be in another restaurant. I pushed my salad plate aside and cut into my steak. It was brown inside. I grabbed the waitress's apron as she was hurrying by and said, "I ordered blood rare. This is well done."

Without a word, she picked up my plate and left. Laura laughed. "That should give you at least a half hour to finish your salad."

I finally got my rare steak, but Laura was already through with her dinner and having coffee. In two hours, the only thing that arrived at our table on time was the bill. I reached for it, but she said, "Let me. Remember, I'm suddenly rich." But I noticed she was a little nervous about using her new money and paid with her credit card. And when she came to the section for the tip, she drew a line through it so the waitress would know she hadn't just overlooked it.

We walked out onto the crowded sidewalk, and someone cut the strap on Laura's purse, and suddenly, it was gone. As he went running down the street, she yelled, "Stop him! He took my purse!"

I started to laugh and said, "Well, that sure settles your moral dilemma for you. Why don't you chase after him and give him that other twenty, also. I'd rather he get caught with it than you."

But she had a better idea. She walked back into the restaurant to our still uncleared table and left the twenty as a well-deserved tip.

17. *Inner Speak*

Most people are bilingual. We don't start out that way, of course. First, we slowly learn the language of those who are caring for us. That is sufficient for most of our early childhood until we start noticing that some of the things we say will get us in trouble. If we want to live a life with the minimum of setbacks and bruises, we must create another language. It is nonvocal, and I call it Inner Speak. Many times, the things we say out loud in our first language are in direct conflict with Inner Speak.

Haven't you ever laughed at a joke that your boss told that was not funny? Or how about the classic question asked by the wife, "Does this make me look fat?"

Is there a husband alive who has not learned by now that the only safe answer to that question is, "No"?

Let me give you an example of how Inner Speak kept me out of much trouble early in my marriage. My mother-in-law was a loving but very bossy woman. When visiting, she would sit in the kitchen and watch me prepare the meals. She wouldn't help; she would just sit there saying things like, "Oh, is that how you do that?" or "Do you know how I would do that?"

My Inner Speak would instantly kick in and say, *No, you old bat, I don't know. But I'll bet you're going to tell me.*

In later years, she and I became very close friends, which I don't think would have happened if I hadn't had this safety valve for my anger.

Perhaps the best example I could give you as to the benefits of developing Inner Speak to smooth your way through life would be to tell you a story. This is nothing new; in fact, it is a story that is played out almost every night of the week in some town somewhere.

The scene is the Happy Hour Cocktail Lounge. The time is 1:00 am. Our lady, let's call her Gladys, is sitting on a stool at the bar taking small sips from her wine glass. Our man enters. We'll call him Charlie. He stops and peers around the dimly lit room. At this hour, there are some couples sitting at the tables, and a few men are at one end of the bar watching basketball replays. At the other end of the bar, he sees the lone figure of our lady. He approaches and says, "Excuse me, is this seat taken?"

His Inner Speak says, *If you have a husband or boyfriend in the men's room, let me know and I'll move on.*

Gladys looks up, smiles, and says, "No, please sit down." Inner Speak: *Thank God, I feel like a fool sitting here by myself. I'll kill Dorothy tomorrow for going off with that guy and leaving me alone.*

Charlie slides onto the stool. "Gimme a scotch rocks, bartender, and another wine for the lady." He turns and smiles. Inner Speak: *Ouch. Up close, she doesn't look all that great. Maybe I'll just drink up and leave.*

Gladys says, "Well, thank you. I was here with a friend,

but she had to leave, so I was just going to finish this. But, if you insist." And she smiles flirtatiously. Inner Speak: *He's not much to look at, a little too short and fat for my taste. But he sure beats sitting here alone.*

Charlie finishes his drink, but doesn't leave as he'd planned. He looks at his watch and turns to Gladys. "I have a friend who plays the piano bar a few blocks from here. If we leave now, we could still catch a few tunes before closing time." Inner Speak: *What is that old joke about every woman looking beautiful at 2:00 am?*

Gladys says, "Oh, that sounds like fun. If it isn't too far." Inner Speak: *Let's face it, girl, nothing better is going to walk in at this time of night.*

And so our two players leave the bar. She smiles and takes his arm, and he walks jauntily along, somehow feeling a little taller.

If these two lonely people hadn't been able to hide their real thoughts through Inner Speak, this little romance would have died way back when he said, "Is this seat taken?"

18. *Fear*

I have only one major, paralyzing fear, and that is the fear of heights. But strangely enough, when it really interferes with my plans, I have found a way to circumvent it and sort of trick it into temporarily going away. For instance, when I have to fly, I get an aisle seat and I sit there, read my book, and avoid looking out the window. I am able to fool myself into thinking we never left the ground. I can go up to the top floor of a high-rise with no trepidation, once again staying away from the windows. But you couldn't pay me enough money to get me to the top of the Empire State Building because the whole purpose of the ride up is to look over the edge. Once I did that, there is no way I could pretend to myself that I was still on the ground floor.

One of the most frightening experiences of my life occurred many years ago in San Francisco. I was with a group of friends, and we decided to have a drink at a bar that was at the top of one of the buildings. This was no problem for me. Once again, I'd just ignore the window view. We got into the elevator and started up. What I didn't know was that this elevator was only inside the building for the first ten floors. Then it continued climbing on the outside of the building. I was standing there chatting with my friends, leaning against the back railing, when suddenly, we were in blinding sunlight. What I thought were solid walls were actually glass, and through them, I could see San Francisco spread out wa-ay down below me. I quickly moved away from the railing, but I didn't want my friends to know of my terror or they'd tease me forever. I felt cold and dizzy, and my heart was pumping wildly. We kept climbing, and I could now see the hills of Oakland and Berkeley across the bay. We were so high up by this time, I was sure the next thing in view would be the New York skyline. My friends were chattering away and pointing out landmarks to each other. I stared at the floor to keep from seeing the ever-widening vista through the glass, but it was too late for this little game to work. My brain already knew full well that I was dangling out there like a cable car in the Alps.

When we finally reached the top and the door opened, my legs were so wobbly I could hardly walk. We sat down at the bar, and I was never so glad to have a drink in my life. In fact, I had two drinks because I remembered that I had to ride that elevator back down again.

19. *A Second Chance*

          I had been sitting in front of the fire for so long that I was almost asleep. Suddenly, I was aware of a small man sitting cross-legged on the floor facing me. I sat up and looked frantically around for some kind of a weapon, and he laughed. "You flatter me, madam. I am far too old to rape and pillage."

"Who are you? What do you want?"

"My name is not important. I am just a spirit who roams through the countryside. But I must tell you that tonight, I am very bored. I would love to find someone to play with. You look like you have a pretty comfortable life here. Tell me, is your life as perfect as it looks?"

"What business is it——"

"Now, now, let me have a little fun. I can do things you

cannot even imagine. With a snap of my fingers, I could take you out of this life and put you into another one."

I was wide awake now and more curious than frightened. He held his hand out, and a cigarette appeared between his fingers. With a finger from his other hand, he lit it. All the while, he was watching me.

"You can quit showing off. I don't allow smoking in my house." The cigarette disappeared, but he had made his point. I was listening.

He said, "I have an idea that's always fun. You pick one thing in your life that you wish you could do over, and I'll let you go back and change it. But you'll have to stay at that point and relive your life from there."

"That's not bad." I laughed. "Assuming you *could* do this. Since I'd know what was ahead, I could avoid all kinds of bad decisions."

"No! You can only change one thing, but that's the delicious part of this game. Changing just one decision could alter your whole life. Want to play? Tell me, if I gave you a second chance, what would you change?"

"That's easy. Just ask my family what I talk about all the time. Years ago, when my children were in school all day, I had hours of time when I could do anything I wanted. And what did I do? I played bridge and shopped and just wasted all those years. I've always wanted to be a writer. Why didn't I use that time to find a job at one of the studios?"

"Well, if that's so important to you, why don't you do it now?"

"Because I'm too old now. They want young writers. And besides, it's different today. That was back when the television industry was fairly new. We lived near the studios, and I could have taken any flunky job they had just to get on board. You can't imagine how it was; the scripts were wonderful. They didn't count on sex or violence to hold the viewers' attention. We had shows like *Matinee Theatre* and *Studio One* ..."

He waved his hand impatiently. "Madam, I don't have to imagine. I was here too. I could take you back in time, and you could get a job. But how do you know you would have been good enough? Or worse, maybe you would have become so successful you would have spent all your time at the office and missed knowing your children as they grew up."

He seemed exasperated. "Do you really want to waste your one request on getting a job? Is this the most important thing you can come up with?"

His disappointment was beginning to give me second thoughts. "I've changed my mind. The worst point in my life so far was going through a divorce. If you really can undo my decisions, then maybe I could marry someone else and be spared all that unhappiness."

"No problem. Let's go back to when you met this gentleman. How old were you?"

"We were both nineteen."

"Yes, I can see him now. What made you decide that you wanted him for a husband?"

"Oh, everything! I was wildly in love with him. He was good-looking, fun loving, and a good dancer."

"I see." he said sarcastically. "Obviously, you used very intelligent standards to judge his potential as a husband and father. So what happened? Did he change?"

"No. That was the problem. When we were twenty-two, we married and were very happy, and by the age of thirty, we had three children. The only problem was that at the age of thirty, he was still a fun-loving kid, and I wanted another adult in the house. I would like to go back and pick out a more mature man to marry."

"Then that's the decision you want to change?"

"Yes. But if you really can do this, how about letting me get rid of some of the other stupid choices I made?"

"I already said no to that. Let's be a little sporting about this, my dear. We've wasted enough time. When I snap my fingers, you will be twenty-two again and can find someone more suitable to marry. But remember, I warned you; this will change the whole rest of your life."

At that, I panicked. "Wait! Wait!" I screamed. It suddenly occurred to me that my children have half their genes from their father. If I married someone else, they would not be the same wonderful children they are now, and I couldn't bear that.

"Madam, please hurry. I am tiring of this. Do you want another husband or not?"

"No! No! Go back to my first wish. Let me try to be a writer!"

He snapped his fingers.

*   *   *   *   *

I pushed my desk chair back and gazed out the window at the tops of the trees in the nearby park. And I thought about my latest screenplay, which had won awards for everyone connected with the show. Normally, this would energize me, and even though it was past the dinner hour, I would still be working but not today. This morning, when I was coming out of my driveway, my next-door neighbor, Mary Ann, waved at me. She was picking flowers, and I knew she was gathering them to put on the table for the bridge luncheon she was having. I couldn't help feeling a little jealous. How nice to have nothing to do every day but shop or play bridge.

I wonder if she knows how lucky she is.

20. Movie Flaws

Kay and Olivia and I had been watching an old rerun of *Magnum PI.* I'd always liked this show, but tonight, I was feeling a little cross.

"Why don't the filmmakers give us credit for having any intelligence? Just look at the basic premise here. We have a man who earns his living doing secret surveillance work, and what does he use when he follows people? A bright red convertible with the top down."

Kay laughed. "Why stop there? I think the so-called thrillers are the worst. Can you name one movie you've seen where you would have been as reckless or as stupid as the heroine?"

Olivia spoke up. "I saw another one of those 'Who's there?' movies the other night."

"What's that?"

"Oh, you know, a 'Who's there?' movie is one where the

heroine is upstairs, all alone in her house, and she hears a noise. She goes to the head of the stairs with a candle or flashlight, peers into the darkness below, and calls out, 'Who's there?'"

We all laughed, and Kay added, "It doesn't even have to be in her house. Let's say she's walking home alone late at night and of course cutting through the woods when she hears footsteps behind her. What would *you* do?"

"I'd run like hell."

"Not our heroine. She stops, turns around with a look of terror, and calls out, 'Who's there?'"

"Yeah," said Kay, "as if the bad guy is going to answer, 'It's just me—the deranged killer.'"

I said, "Let's get back to our heroine's house. Let's say she's being stalked. Does she call the police? Does she go to a friend's house? No, she goes home alone. Once there, does she lock all doors and windows, run upstairs, and lock herself in her bedroom? Tell me, Kay, what's the first thing she'll do?"

"Well, when she gets upstairs, she'll take all her clothes off, of course, so she can get in a shower or bubble bath."

"That's exactly what I mean. Just once, I wish that we could see a movie showing how intelligent people would really act in a time of danger. But the only way that would happen would be if we wrote the script ourselves."

I liked that idea. "Why *don't* we write our own script? Olivia, do you still see that girl who writes for the *Mystery Hour* show?"

"Well, yeah, but ..."

"Let's write a story that shows how real people handle real situations. And while we're at it, let's get rid of all the stupid situations that are copied from one show to the next. Do you think your friend would be interested?"

"I doubt it. But let's do it anyway. It would make me feel good just to read it. I'll even give you a name for it. Let's call it *'Bye-Bye, Cliché.'*"

We each got to work separately, helped by an occasional sip of wine, and giggled as we kept getting new thoughts.

"Oh, we've *got* to have a funeral scene. Talk about clichés! Every movie funeral takes place in pouring rain with the people standing around holding those huge black umbrellas. Our first cliché breaker will be a funeral on a bright sunny day with the birds chirping."

"Okay, and when our hero and heroine leave the cemetery, they discover they're being followed by two bad guys who begin shooting at them. Well, the driver pretty much has to sit up far enough that he can see over the wheel, but I'm tired of watching chases where the passenger victim also sits upright, making a perfect target as she keeps turning to look back in horror at the bad guys. In our movie, she will duck down like any five-year-old kid would have sense enough to do."

"Here's another scene we see a lot, how about those chases in underground garages? The bad guys are in a car, and the hero is on foot. He runs in a straight line down the middle of the garage until they run him down. In *our* script, the minute the car takes after him, he'll dodge behind the pillars, and if they follow him, they will crash. End of chase."

"Shall we have a Bogart-type detective in our movie?"

"Yeah, but his office will be very neat, and he won't have a bottle of whisky in the bottom drawer. When the heroine comes in for help, he is sitting there working a crossword puzzle. With a pen."

Olivia cut in, "Let me do the scene where the heroine comes in to ask him for help. She's really plain looking, with thick glasses and her hair pulled back into a tight bun. So somewhere during the conversation, he rudely says, 'Do you need those glasses?' which of course she doesn't, and he takes them off. Then, excited beyond belief, he reaches back and takes one pin out of her hair. A huge mass of hair comes tumbling down around her shoulders. He steps back to view her and says, 'I don't understand it, you're *still* plain.'"

By the end of the evening, our wish to finally create just one intelligent scary movie had been granted. But Olivia didn't want to show it to her friend at the studio, because we all had to admit that it was totally boring. That was the answer: Hollywood learned long ago that stupid people are much more fun to watch.

So, the next time you see a scantily clad lady stand at the top of the stairs and call out, "Who's there?" just remember, if she called the police instead, the movie would soon end, and you'd want your money back.

21. Life with the Rich and Famous

One day, I was in Southern California visiting my cousin and while waiting for her to get off work, I walked down Hollywood Boulevard to see what strange sights were around. Usually, when I do that, I find myself looking mostly at other tourists looking back at me to see if I am anyone they might recognize. An eager sidewalk salesman stuck a flyer into my hands. It said they were having tryouts for a new game show. I went to the address given and so did hundreds of others.

We went into a room, and the big crowd of people very soon was whittled down to just a few dozen by two men at the door who went down the line saying yes or no, and the rejected would sadly depart.

My cousin is a waitress and gets occasional bit parts. She says the secret to a television audition is animation. Never mind what you say, just be the perkiest, happiest person in the room. Boy was I perky, and I was one of the ones chosen to appear that night on a show with eleven others. I still didn't know what it was about but didn't really care. The emcee explained to us and the audience that we were going to be given a sort of pretend million dollars. We had to spend it all the next day, and in just one store. We were assigned guides who would drive us wherever we wanted to shop and who would explain the contest to the store owner. Tomorrow night, we would return to the show. The contestant who had made the cleverest, most original purchases would be given the actual money to complete the sale. A panel from tomorrow's audience would decide.

My guide was named Albert, and he didn't look like he thought following me around would be much fun. He asked where I wanted to go, but I told him to wait. We sat in his car for a long time while I tried to think. What would be a smarter purchase than any of the other contestants would think of? We could go straight to a jewelry store and invest the whole million in probably five minutes. But that seemed so obvious, it would never win. I thought about a car dealer. Were there any cars worth a million? I doubted it, but what did I know was my only car was a twelve-year-old Volkswagen. I thought about furs. Again, too obvious.

Then I thought about a house. Out-of-towners read movie magazines that talk about the beautiful mansions the movie stars lived in. Now I had the money to buy one! And the best part was that maybe the rest of the contestants wouldn't think of a realtor's office as a store!

I turned to Albert who was so bored he looked like he was asleep. I shook him. "I decided what I want to buy. Take me to the nearest real estate office."

"Wait a minute," said Albert "you're supposed to buy things from a *store*."

"Well now, Albert, what is a store? It is a commercial building full of things that people want to sell. Like houses."

He couldn't argue with that and drove us to a large Beverly Hills real estate office. He gave a letter that explained the TV program to the broker who greeted us, and she said she had several homes in my price range. She tapped a few keys on her computer and said, "Here's a listing for a mil that just came on the market."

She swung the monitor around so I could see the listing. I was confused. I was looking at a picture of a small, very ordinary ranch-style house. What was this? Was this all you could buy in Beverly Hills for a million dollars?

But I wasn't going to give up. Calling a real estate office a store was too good an idea. I said, "I don't suppose you might have a teensy little house owned by a movie star, would you?"

At that, the realtor said, "As a matter of fact, I do. The Olga Harmony house is on the market. They are asking a mil five, but I think for a quick cash deal, they'd take a mil."

I thought I was pretty familiar with most of the stars; maybe this was a new one? I said, "Who's Olga Harmony? I'm afraid I haven't heard of her."

"At one time, she was famous all over the world."

"Well, what has she been in that I might have seen?"

"Her greatest period was during the silent movie days."

"You mean she's not the one who's selling it?"

The realtor laughed. "Oh no, she's been dead for about fifty years."

"But you said it was her house?"

"That's what we do, dear. If a famous star owns a home, it is forever referred to as her home no matter how many people own it after she is gone."

I was disappointed. But according to the realtor, this was a movie star's house, which should give me some points. And my time was running out.

"May I see it?" I asked, and the realtor turned her computer screen so I could see the tiny picture at the top. The listing said Spanish style, but there were so many bushes covering it, it was hard to tell. "Could I go over and see it? I can't tell anything by this picture."

"I'm sorry, but they won't give me a key. They're at their Palm Springs house now, but they'll be back tomorrow."

I looked at Albert and said, "What'll I do?"

"You don't have a whole lotta time, you know. You have to buy something today, so if you want it, looks like you'll have to make an offer without looking at it."

I turned back to the realtor and said, "Can you write up the offer and fax it to your client? Tell him if he doesn't accept today, I can't buy it. But let him know, if the audience doesn't pick me, this cancels the deal."

The realtor said, "Before we go any further, why don't I see if I can reach him by phone?"

She called and explained the deal to the current owner who thought this whole thing was ridiculous—and, I thought, with good reason. She suggested to him that he sell it to me "as is" in return for coming down to a million dollars. She turned to me and said, "Is that okay?"

"Sure," I said. What did I care? It wasn't *my* money.

She got a fax number from him where she could send my offer and asked him to fax his acceptance immediately. So I had a done deal and woke Albert up to tell him.

The next night on television was somewhat of a blur to me. The other contestants and I showed up and took turns telling what we had purchased. One man had almost bought out an electronics store with huge wall TVs and computers and announced to the audience that he was donating them to the needy. An obvious pitch to the judges, and we all glared at him. And I was right about the jewelry store as two contestants had purchased a dazzling array of bracelets and rings. When it was my turn, I said I'd gone to a real estate store, and the audience laughed. Then I told them my purchase wasn't just an ordinary house; it had been owned by the world-famous movie star Olga Harmony. The audience applauded, and I wondered how many of them had even heard of her.

The panel of judges thought my choice of stores was the most original, so I was given the money to complete the sale.

The next day, the seller returned and let me see the house. It was not only not a mansion; it was barely even a livable house. No wonder he spent his time at Palm Springs. It was probably lovely when Miss Olga Harmony was alive and entertaining her show-business friends. But nothing had been updated and the garden had grown like a jungle, completely enveloping the property.

Since I didn't have to get a loan, I had a very quick escrow, and when I moved in, I spent a week chopping the jungle down and sort of enjoying my new digs. After all, here was little me, living in Beverly Hills, and don't forget, the house was *free*! But the floor furnace needed replacing, and I found spots where the roof had leaked. But I didn't have the money for repairs. And let's not forget the $10,000 in property taxes I would have to come up with each year. So I didn't plan for a very long stay.

A lot of my friends and relatives had seen me on that television show and wanted to come visit me, but I kept putting them off. How was I going to explain to them that all one million dollars buys in California is a fixer-upper? My cousin thought the whole adventure was hilarious, and when I moved in and started trying to make improvements, she would come over and just sit and laugh.

Well, let her tease all she wants. I may be naïve, but I'm a quick learner. I'm going to splash some paint on the walls, put an ad in the paper selling it as a "movie star's home," and then just sit here and wait for some starstruck out-of-towner to come along and take it off my hands.

22. *A Reluctant Traveler*

I thought that picking a spot for an ideal vacation would be easy, as there are so many foreign countries that I haven't seen. But wait a minute; it would have to be one that is not at war, if I want a peaceful stay. But which one? If the country I pick is not at war, how do I know it will stay that way after my plane lands?

And speaking of planes, air travel is beginning to scare me. This past year, I flew up north for a family gathering, and I had a child's toy in my carry-on bag. The toy was filled with tiny metal objects. I left it unwrapped so when it set the machine off, I could show them that it was simply a toy for a three-year-old. But when I walked through the line and my carry-on set off the machine, the inspector did nothing but stare at it. Then she waved to another inspector, and they both looked at it through the x-ray machine. Meanwhile, it sat there setting off all the bells and whistles. The conveyer belt had stopped, and the people were piling up in line behind me. I kept saying to myself, *Well, open it, dummy.*

Then the man said, "Oh, the machine's probably broken again," and they both laughed and sent the bag on its way. So you can see how tight security is. But what the heck, even if they strip us all naked and dump everything out of our carry-ons, what difference does it make? We still get in the plane and sit on top of the huge cargo hold which is filled with suitcases and boxes that aren't even x-rayed.

So I decided against taking a plane, which leaves out most foreign countries unless I go by ship. I could take a cruise ship. At least that would have been an option up until recently. But did you read about those pirates that tried to hijack a cruise ship off the coast of Africa? No, no cruise ship for me.

I always wanted to take a long train trip, like that American Orient Express. But a woman I know took a train trip back east last Christmas, and a couple of the cars slid right off the tracks. She wasn't hurt, but she didn't come back a train enthusiast either.

Okay, so who needs long-distance transportation? Southern California brags about being a place where one can drive from the desert to the sea in just a few hours.

I ruled out the desert almost immediately. Have you seen the snakes and scorpions out there? I'd be shaking my shoes out every morning and afraid to walk or even sit anywhere.

I think I would prefer the beach. There is nothing more hazardous in the sand than cigarette butts. But on second thought, I shouldn't go to the beach. I would have to hide under a huge hat, an umbrella, and at least a number 1000 sunscreen. And if I'm that covered up, what am I doing on the beach? I surely wouldn't be swimming or even wading. Have you forgotten *Jaws*?

I should have realized what my decision would be. I would stay home. I would tell all my friends that I was going on vacation and then draw the blinds, not answer the phone, and just lie around doing nothing.

I would finally have time to read the latest books. I would listen to my big-band music from the forties. And I would eat anything in my freezer that only needed microwaving.

This, to me, would be an ideal vacation. But of course I would have an emergency suitcase packed and near the back door—just in case there was an earthquake.

23. My Addiction

I have successfully fought the demons of cigarettes and liquor. My only current addiction is a very pleasurable one that I have no desire to cure. I am a member of that vast army of crossword-puzzle workers, hereinafter referred to as CPWs.

This craving is easy to feed. My morning paper contains the *New York Times* crossword, and I don't put it away until it is completely solved. I also subscribe to two different publications that send me weekly crosswords. I bring them with me on plane trips, to doctors' offices, and any place where I have to kill time. Unlike books, you can pick them up and put them down without having to remember the plot.

I always tell non-CPWs that this is not a waste of time. Crosswords not only increase your vocabulary, but they improve your spelling, as just one wrong letter will block your solution. In recent years, I have read articles that claim that exercising your brain, such as in working crosswords, will help to stave off

Alzheimer's. I tell this to my doubting friends, but of course, it won't do much good. Because when I am old and mentally sharp, they will be too addled to remember what I said.

But I must confess to stretching things a bit. True, puzzles do increase your vocabulary, but mostly with words that are only found in other puzzles, not words that you ever hear spoken out in the real world. I saw a cartoon that showed an animal sitting in a cage in the zoo with a sign saying "Ibex." Underneath the name on this cage was written, "Only found in crossword puzzles."

A friend of mine told me about a trick he played on a boy he went to college with. They lived in the same dorm, and this boy was the only one in the building who actually subscribed to a newspaper. The reason for his subscription was because he liked to work the morning crossword before going to his first class. The paper usually arrived about 4:00 am. One night, my friend set his alarm early, and when the paper was delivered, he sneaked down the hall and brought it back to his room. He very carefully unfolded it, and then he and his roommate got to work. They finished the puzzle, carefully refolded the paper, and put it back in the hall. I can well imagine the bewilderment and disappointment of this poor student who eagerly pulled out the crossword only to find the answers already penciled in. My friend thinks this is hilarious, but as a CPW, I'll bet that somewhere in this world, there is a middle-aged man who still resents the morning that someone spoiled his puzzle. He may even be in therapy.

I should warn you that sometimes a trained CPW's mind can go off in the wrong direction. When I was a young bride, the phone rang one morning. I answered and a man's voice said, "Is Greg there?"

I told him no, that my husband was at the office. He then made a couple of rather strange remarks, which I ignored. I thought he had a very gross sense of humor. But since I assumed he was a friend of my husband, I was totally off guard.

It didn't occur to me that he could get my husband's first name simply by looking at our telephone listing.

Well, I guess he got impatient at my lack of response and decided to get to the point, because suddenly, he said, "I've got something here you'd really like. I'll give you a hint. It has five letters, and it starts with the letter 'P.'" Well, this was right down my alley.

"I know!" I said triumphantly. "Pizza!"

That was many years ago, but I think I still hold the record for being the only woman who ever had an obscene caller hang up on her.

24. Be Careful What You Say in Front of the Dead

I was at a funeral recently, and I actually heard one of the guests say something rather catty about the deceased. I was shocked. Generally, even if you're not overly fond of someone, you manage to find something civil to say at the funeral. We were next to the casket, and I couldn't help wondering if the deceased could somehow hear her. And I could envision the following scenario.

*   *   *   *   *

I can't believe that I am actually lying here in the visitation room, looking out. I always thought dead was dead, but apparently, it is taking my brain awhile to slow down and stop. Must be all those crossword puzzles I worked. I read once that they keep your brain alert. But this is ridiculous.

Amelia and Helen are here. I can hear them across the room. They are apparently arranging things for the guests. I

84

wonder who will come? What will they say about me? Amelia and Helen are my dearest friends. If either were to remember me with just one word, I wonder what it would be.

I was so fortunate to have them in my life. Amelia and I were instant friends in school and all through the years. And then, when I hired Helen as my housekeeper, to my surprise, she became much more and almost as dear a friend as Amelia. I was an only child, and I never married, so they have really been all the family I ever had.

This came up in a very important way one day when an attorney who was doing some minor legal work for me asked me if I had a will. I told him, "No, never thought about it." He said without a will, I would die intestate. I laughed. "Intestate? Is that some kind of disease?"

"Pay attention to what I'm trying to tell you. If you die intestate, it means you not only don't have a will, you don't have any relatives. In that case, all of your property will revert to the state of California."

I didn't like that. Those guys in Sacramento had enough of my money; I sure didn't want to give them any more. He wanted to draw up my will, of course, but I decided to save the money and write the will myself. I got a book out of the library and learned how to write a holographic will, so I not only didn't have to pay a lawyer; I didn't need any witnesses and didn't even need to have it notarized.

The will was kind of fun. Amelia and Helen would get it all, of course, and I spent a whole day itemizing the particular things around the house I wanted to leave to each one. Then I would have them split the financial side of my estate in half. But I wouldn't show it to them; I would leave it as a wonderful surprise. The voices are louder now, and Helen's face is right above me.

"I don't like the way she looks. They used too much makeup; the lipstick is too dark; and look at her hair. This makeup guy must work on aging movie stars!"

Well, I don't like that. Bad enough to be dead, but apparently, I've been made up to look like Norma Desmond!

"What happened to her tea set, Helen? It wasn't on her buffet this morning."

"I have it at home. I had a luncheon over the weekend, and I knew she'd never miss it."

"Well, please bring it right back. I'm sure she left everything to me. After all, I was her best friend."

"Don't worry, Amelia. If she really wants you to have it, she'll say so in her will."

"What will? I never saw a will. You know how senile she was. She probably just *thought* she made one out."

Hey, what do you mean senile? My memory is as good as yours, Amelia, and yes, as a matter of fact, I *did* leave you the tea set, but I didn't expect you to take possession before my funeral! How about a little grieving here, ladies?

Helen is hovering over me now, fussing with my hair. "Amelia, I'm a little concerned about your attitude about that tea set. Does that mean you and I are going to fight over every single thing she has?"

"Like I said, Helen, let's read the will. As soon as the funeral is over, let's go through her desk and see if we can find it."

"I don't care about that damned tea set. There are a lot more valuable things than that lying around the house. If we don't find a will, I'm just going to clear out a few things I know very well she'd want me to have."

"You touch one thing without permission, and I'll go straight to the police. I am the one who was her closest, dearest friend. I went on trips with her. I spent an awful lot of time with her all these years. And a lot of it was pretty boring."

"So did I. I was there every single day taking care of that monstrous old house. I did a lot more for her than you did."

"Yes, my dear, but you were a servant and pretty well paid. How long would you have stuck around for free?"

"No longer than you would have, if you didn't think you'd be her sole heir."

My two dearest friends, and all they can think of is who will get what. Up until now, I would have guessed that the one word either of them might use to describe me might be *loving* or, hopefully, *fun* or maybe *interesting*. Now it sounds like their first adjective might be *rich*. Was that all I was to them? I paid Helen a generous salary because I could afford to, but also because I loved and needed her. And I took Amelia on cruises with me, took her to many places she never could have afforded, because I loved her company. But was that why she remained such a close friend? Was it just my *things* that were important to these two?

I wonder why Helen hasn't seen my will. Every morning before she arrived, I typed up a complete list of what I wanted done around the house, what meals I wanted, and everything I could think of to keep my home running smoothly. I put this list in an envelope and left it on the corner of my desk for her to find. Yesterday, I didn't feel well, and somehow, I had a premonition about my death. I don't know why. I had been ill for a long time, but this felt different——and final. So I got out my will, put it in an envelope, and left it in place of the note I usually left for Helen. And I thought about what a wonderful surprise I was leaving for her and Amelia.

Now I'm sorry I wrote that will. I am so hurt by their coldness and greed, I think I would *rather* my property go to the state——*anywhere* but to them. But it is too late for me to do anything about it now.

Helen's voice interrupted my thoughts. "Amelia, remember all of her famous daily directives?"

"You mean those long notes she left for you every morning?"

"Yes, like I was too stupid to run the house after thirty years? Well, when I got there yesterday, the doctor was already there, and he told me she had died during the night, and could

I take care of the arrangements? I went into the den, and there was one of those familiar little envelopes to program my day. Do you know what I did? I put it through the paper shredder and declared my independence!"

I can scarcely believe my good luck. Thank you, Helen. For the rest of your lives, I'll bet the adjective you and Amelia will probably use the most when you think of me is *intestate*.

25. Igor's Travels

My great-aunt Ida kept a brass gargoyle about six inches tall on her coffee table among all her fern plants. No one in my family remembers where it came from. It is quite ugly. My older brother Joel called it "Igor," and when I was little, he would tell me stories about hearing Igor moan. Once, he told me Igor walked around when no one was there. Because of this, I never would go into her living room unless someone else was there.

I was a teenager when Great Aunt Ida died. When her will was read, everyone was surprised that she had specified that she wanted me to have her beloved gargoyle. She had actually gone to her lawyer and added a special codicil to this effect. I asked my mother why and she said, "Apparently, Ida thought that you were extremely fond of it."

"No!" I wailed. "I hate that ugly thing!"

Joel just stood there grinning at me. Then I figured it

out. He was the one who had told her I loved that gargoyle. I was too old to be scared by Igor anymore, so Joel had found another way to torment me. I didn't want to upset my mother, so I dropped the subject. I went into my bedroom closet, moved a couple of shoeboxes, and shoved Igor way into the back of the shelf so I couldn't see his ugly face. Joel went back to college, and I kind of forgot about Igor until Joel came home again for Thanksgiving vacation. I didn't mention Igor once during his stay. Then, the day he was leaving, I wrapped that gargoyle inside of a sock and hid it way down inside Joel's backpack.

A week later, the doorbell rang, and a package sat on the doormat addressed to me. I opened it to find, of course, Igor. It was December, so I wrapped it back up, added some decorations, and a few weeks later put it under our tree. Joel laughed when he opened it, but Mother said, "I wish you children would stop this silliness. Ida really loved that gargoyle."

But this was only the beginning of our endless game. One of my more inspired moments was when I stuck it to him at the stag party thrown before his wedding. His best man, Tim, was also a good friend of mine. So he helped me give Igor back. Since I couldn't be there, Tim took a picture of it for me. When they wheeled the cake into the room, and the stripper jumped out, she was holding Igor. The expression on my brother's face was priceless.

Through the years, the game didn't stop, but it slowed down. When Joel married, he moved five hundred miles north. I eventually finished college and married and ended up moving south. Suddenly, we were one thousand miles apart. And we were busy working and raising our families. Several years would pass, and then Igor would surface again. What had started out as a couple of teenagers playing "Tag, you're it!" has evolved into a lifelong joke.

Today, we are both senior citizens. That grinning little

creep has been sitting in the back of my closet shelf for a couple of years now. It's about time he went on another trip.

This gargoyle that I didn't want has added an unexpected bonus to my life. Some siblings drift apart in their later years, but this foolishness has caused Joel and me to become, and remain, very good friends.

And just think of all the frequent-flier miles that Igor has piled up!

26. *Expiration Date*

It was late afternoon, and I was in the cemetery at my mother's grave. I went there on the first week of every month to leave a little bouquet of flowers and trim any weeds that had started to grow over her plot. This particular afternoon, I sat and stared at the stone. Below her name, it gave the year of her birth and the year of her death. And I found myself wondering what it would be like if, when we came into this world, we not only knew our birth date, but our death date as well. Would this be a good thing to know or bad?

I was suddenly aware that I was not alone. I looked up to see an elderly man standing beside me. He said, "I have watched you come here month after month, waiting for you to ask yourself that question."

"Excuse me?" I said, a little startled, as the two of us were all alone on this hillside.

"You were wondering if people should know their death dates."

"How did you ...?" I began, but he interrupted.

"Actually, I have told this to many of you. But you have to ask. You have to want to know."

I picked up my purse and started to get up. I wanted to get away from this strange man.

"Relax," he said, "if I had wanted to harm you, I most surely could have a long time ago. I just came over because your thoughts tell me that maybe you are ready to know when you are going to die."

"Who are you?"

"Who I am doesn't matter," he said. "But knowing your death date can make a great difference in how you live. I want you to go home and think about this. When you come back next month, let me know." And he seemed to disappear before my eyes.

By the time I got home, I was ready to believe that I had imagined the whole thing. But his proposition intrigued me. What a difference it would make if we all knew how long we had to live.

I thought of my mother-in-law. When I was first married, I noticed that everyone catered to her because, I was told, she was frail. She had a pretty good thing going back then. But now, everyone who waited on her has been dead for a long time, and she—at the age of 109—is still around. When I visit her now, I think of her poor husband, who hired a housekeeper and a cook when they could not really afford it, because he thought that she was too frail to do her own housework. I wonder how he would have acted if he'd known that she would outlive him by over fifty years.

If we all arrived with an expiration date, probate attorneys would have a hard time finding clients. In their final years, wealthy people could slowly transfer their assets to their heirs, leaving just enough for burial expenses.

By the time I went to bed that night, I could think of nothing but advantages in knowing my death date. And I thought of a plane trip I had coming up. I have always had a fear of flying, but now I wouldn't have to be afraid. If I didn't fly on my death date, I would be all right. Then I sat up in bed.

But what if it's the pilot's day to die? Wouldn't he take all of us down with him? I would have to check this with that little man at the cemetery.

The worst scenario of all didn't hit me until the following morning. What if I said yes, I wanted to know, and the answer was that I was going to die in six days? What would I do?

I would want to call my children and grandchildren and ask them all to come over at once, even though they are busy with their own lives. At the same time, I would want to book that trip to Europe that I had put off for ten years. And I would want to fly to San Francisco to see my best friend, Irene. She is my best friend, why don't I see her more often? I thought of so many things I had put off that I probably would waste precious days just trying to make up my mind what to do first. And in what would seem like seconds, that sixth day would arrive, and I would be gone. But would my last week have been happy? I don't think so. All that frantic rushing around does not seem like a pleasant way to spend my final days.

The next month as I drove to the cemetery, I thought what a silly fool I was … There *was* no such creature who could tell me my death date. Yet he had made such an impression on me that the weekend after I saw him, I was in San Francisco visiting with Irene, and we agreed that we would never again let so much time go by without seeing each other. I was leaving the next morning for my very first European tour. So even if he didn't exist, he had really changed my way of living.

I walked over to the grave with my flowers and sat down. Moments later, he appeared. "Well?" he said.

"I decided against it."

"This is your only chance, my dear. Are you sure?"

"Yes, I'm sure. I'm going to start doing what I want while I still have time. I just don't think I would be happy knowing exactly how *much* time."

I looked up to see his reaction, but he was already gone.

27. *Shifting Gears*

Occasionally, the newspapers carry a sad story about an elderly person who loses control of his car, running down and hurting or killing pedestrians. I'm going to tell you a story about an elderly woman—me, to be precise—who used a moment such as this to propel herself onto the front page of newspapers all over the world and who even today is considered to be a national heroine.

It started very inauspiciously, as most historic events do. I was coming home from a writing class I was taking. I was hot and tired and wanted something cold to drink. I spotted a coffee shop, but a road crew was creating quite a traffic jam in front of it. Cars had to swerve around them while they stood around an open manhole. I somehow found my way through the cones and parked and went in.

I had just purchased a new car, and everything in it was quite different from what I was used to. There were strange icons on the dashboard, and the gears seemed to be in all the wrong places. When I put it in what would have been reverse in my old car, the windshield wipers would turn on and a glass cleaner would start spraying. On this fatal day, when I came back out of the coffee shop, I saw a break in the traffic. Quickly, I started the car and attempted to make a fast exit. But instead of "drive," I had put it into"reverse." The car shot backwards, bumping over the curb, heading straight for the four street workers. I could feel the bumps as my car knocked them sprawling. I looked in my rearview mirror in horror as I saw the close-up of a face as one of the men disappeared under my car, and I felt two more bumps as my car went up and over him.

I didn't know what to do. I slammed on the brake, turned off the motor, and sat there shaking. Someone yelled at me to back up and get the car out of the way, so I turned the motor back on and tried to put it in reverse, which of course, cleaned my windshield again. So someone removed me, not too gently, from the car and drove it out of the way. Police cars and ambulances appeared and took the victims away. The police questioned me and began examining the accident scene.

Meanwhile, at the hospital, all hell had broken loose. One worker was much taller than the others. And when they removed the helmet and clothing from his body, a Muslim hospital aide screamed, fell to the floor, and began praying. Others came running in, and soon, there was a large crowd around his bed. In a short time, a positive identification was made. One of the men I killed was Osama bin Laden. Trained agents from all over the world had been searching for him. During all this time, had he been fixing potholes in the San Fernando Valley?

Television news crews pulled into the parking lot. Back at the scene of the accident, everyone had been cleared away and was awaiting the bomb squad. There was evidence that the men were wiring the manhole with enough explosives to level the entire city of Encino.

I had been released to go home, where my phone didn't stop ringing. I received calls from Barbara Walters, Larry King, and all the news agencies. Several CIA agents were waiting for me on my front porch. "How had I found him? How had I spotted him?"

I could have told the truth, that I stupidly was in the wrong gear and had no idea who he was. But having just come from the writing class, I thought what a wonderful story this would make. And I found myself saying that yes, I had recognized him and felt I had to act fast before he slipped away.

The stunning news of his death pierced his followers in the Middle East like a dagger. All over Iraq and the surrounding areas, they fled into the mountains to mourn him. The discovery and failure of his bomb plot seemed to take all of the energy out of the terrorist activities. As the days went by, cities such as Baghdad experienced a quiet peace they hadn't known in years. The local residents began venturing out into the streets again. And our troops began returning home.

According to the news accounts, which of course I was poring over, all of this was due to the quick-wittedness of the little old lady who spotted him. I started believing some of this myself and was very proud to read about how I was such an expert driver that I was able to chase him down and foil his getaway while driving in reverse.

I was invited to the White House where I received a Medal of Honor. I would never have the energy or time to answer all of the requests I've had to speak before various groups. And some old guy in Massachusetts wants to sculpt my bust, which sounds pretty personal. All future history books will list my name as the person who found and destroyed Osama bin Laden, totally changing the course of the Middle East.

I love being famous for this, even if I *was* just driving in the wrong gear. And if the fame from this causes me any inconvenience in my private life, who cares? Look at all the troops I got safely home.

28. Do Your Possessions Represent Your Personality?

Charlotte is always taking these magazine quizzes. This one was to find three possessions around your house that would best represent your personality.

My first problem with this quiz was in determining what my personality is. I am too close to see it, so I thought if I wandered around my home, I might discover something about myself.

I started in the basement. After all, that is where I store things, and if they meant enough to me to keep, maybe there would be a clue there as to my character.

I stopped in front of the large poster on the wall. It is from a shooting gallery and shows my feeble attempt to nail the bad guy, as all my bullet holes seem to be around and not on him.

Many years ago, during the Watts Riots, I suddenly realized that there could be a time when rioting might spread to my quiet little town, and if I called 911, the police could be too busy to answer. In that case, it would be up to me to defend myself. So I bought a gun, a Lady Smith, and a box of bullets. I carefully loaded the gun and put it in the drawer next to my bed. I never went to a firing range to learn how to use it; in fact, for years, it had never even been fired. It just sat there quietly next to the Kleenex.

One day, my son decided to take me to a shooting range in spite of my protests. The cement walls and ceiling echoed the noise until to me, it was almost unbearable, but I did the best I could. When I used up the bullets and we pulled the target up close, we discovered that not one hole was in the bad guy's body. I had brought the target home and hung it on the basement wall, and now I wondered what it was saying about my personality. I like to think it shows that I am a courageous woman who lives alone but is not afraid to face the enemy. My son thinks it shows that an intruder might die of old age before I ever hit him.

I went upstairs and into my den. On top of my bookshelf is the goofiest trophy you could ever imagine. It is of a lady bowler, and she is so twisted up you know if she releases the ball, it will not even stay in the lane. The gold strip across the bottom has my name and says that my team came in last place in a tournament. When it was presented to me, I thought it was hilarious and have displayed it in the den ever since. But my partner was so embarrassed that he refused to even walk up and accept his trophy. Maybe this might say a little about my personality. If I am so inept that I come in last place in a sport, I don't mind admitting it. In fact, I will tell everyone about it and laugh right along with them. I knew I was a lousy bowler when I started, and so did my partner. But we were there to have fun, which we did, so why the anguish?

And wait a minute here, is there any connection between

these two possessions? If I take a huge bowling ball and roll it down an alley and miss all ten of those pins that are standing still, how the heck can you expect me to send one tiny bullet through the vital parts of a moving target?

So what had I learned about myself so far? That I am brave and strong, even though my abilities are a little questionable. The first time I ever pull the trigger in fear, I will probably shoot myself in the foot. But a friend told me that there is nothing scarier than a woman with a gun, especially if she is shaking and doesn't know what she is doing. So my shooting range target and gun might show that I am more self-reliant than a lot of senior citizens my age, and my comic bowler being on display shows that I am confident enough in myself that I am not embarrassed by coming in last place in a contest.

I continued hunting. I wanted one more description of my personality.

I phoned one of my daughters and asked her to say something that describes me, and she didn't answer. What would I like her to say? What kind of personality would a mother like her kids to think she has?

The phone rang later. My daughter said, "I decided the way I would describe you would be 'fun to be with.'"

I thought about that. All these years behind me and the best my child could come up with is "fun to be with"? Have I not been her teacher, her comforter, her advisor, and hopefully some kind of good role model?

"What's the matter?" she said. "You sound disappointed. What did you want me to say?"

"I don't know. I don't sound very accomplished if all I am to you kids is someone who's fun to be with."

"But don't you see, Mom, that means we don't come over to your house because of duty. And our kids don't have to be forced to go see you and hug you. We see you because we enjoy being with you. Isn't that important to you?"

"I guess so, when you put it that way."

All morning, I kept thinking about what she said. Wanting to be with someone really has nothing to do with love. I loved my mother, but I can remember how the three weeks she stayed with me each year seemed interminable. We would run out of things to say the first day, and I was always so thankful when I could put her back on the plane to go home.

And everyone loved my grandfather, but he had such strong political views that no one wanted to sit next to him at the table. So I decided that "fun to be with" was really a good compliment and wondered what possession I had in my house to represent it.

In one of my kitchen cupboards is a raft of mugs, and every one has a variation of "Best Mom on Earth." I never used them, but the kids kept bringing them over on holiday occasions, and I didn't like to throw them away. From what my daughter said, apparently, the playful joking always going on around my house was enough to make them want to be there. Well, if all that kidding around makes my children comfortable, I plan to keep it up.

I took a cup from the shelf and added it to my list.

29. *What Happens When the Glamour Fades?*

Most women over sixty see a gradual change in their lives. No matter if she keeps her figure trim or continues to dress stylishly, the world views her in a different light. Maybe it is the first time she walks past a group of men working in the street and not one even gives her a second glance, let alone a whistle. To the people in this world under fifty, she has somehow become invisible. This is a hard mental adjustment to make.

The under-fifties seem to suffer from the same problem. What are they afraid of? The twenties coming up in the world? In the job market, a youthful appearance has come to be more valued than knowledge.

A friend of mine works in a plastic surgery office in

Beverly Hills. He tells me that older women used to be their big customers for tucks and other procedures to stave off the effects of old age. But now, they are doing a brisk business with twenty-year-olds. And women are not the only ones having breast work done. He says that because of all the bare-chested love scenes, a lot of young male actors are running around sporting rippled abs and pecs that are actually implants.

One has to admire Robert Redford and Clint Eastwood whose craggy faces make them look about one hundred years old. But then, they made their money and achieved their power so long ago they can afford to thumb their noses at our youth-obsessed society.

Through the years, countless surveys have shown that people are inclined to give the benefit of the doubt to good-looking people. Teachers give them better grades than plain-looking students, and employers are inclined to hire the better-looking of the applicants who apply.

One day, when I was about forty, I went to a company awards luncheon at a local country club. It was a big deal for my office, and when I won the trophy for tops in sales, my whole table went wild. Friends from all over the room were sending over drinks and congratulating me.

After I left, I had only driven a few blocks before I noticed I was having trouble with my vision. The lane markers up ahead of me kept moving and converging with each other. Too late, I realized I'd had too many drinks and should have asked someone to drive me home. I only lived a few miles away, so all I could think of was to get into the curb lane, drive slowly, and hope no one would notice me. But a few blocks later, there was a red light flashing in my rearview mirror. The policeman came up to my window and asked if I'd been drinking. I said, "Yes," and picked up my trophy to show it to him. I told him about winning my award. I just kept smiling and babbling away because I'd noticed he still hadn't written anything on his ticket pad. He went back to his car and phoned for a cab, which arrived very shortly. I got out, still clutching my trophy, and the policeman locked up my car and put me in the cab for a safe ride home. Remember, I was forty then. If this happened today, the headlines in tomorrow's hometown newspaper would be "Grandmother Spends Night in Drunk Tank."

So yes, we got many favors during that part of our lives when we were young and attractive. And we miss the quicker service and special discounts that we got by flirting. But now, if you senior ladies have to get in line while the cute young girls are being waited on first, just remember that you had your fun.

It's their turn now.

30. Memory Versus Actual Experience

Which is better, the memory of a great experience or the experience itself? There is a big difference. I can give you a good example of when the memory is better: I was present at Dodger Stadium when Sandy Koufax pitched his perfect game. When I would tell that to Dodger fans who had not been there, they would envy me and wish they had been with me. I am glad I witnessed this, I guess, but can you imagine anything more boring than nine innings without a hit?

Many experiences are so exciting or so dangerous that one has only a hazy awareness at the time. A wedding might be an example. The poor bride has been planning and anticipating and arranging details for so long that when the actual event starts to be played out, she is almost unconscious. It is not until later when she calms down that she is able to remember everything, and sometimes not even then. So once again, her memories would be of a beautiful ceremony, but in reality, she almost had to be carried to the altar.

My parents celebrated their twenty-fifth anniversary by taking a two-week cruise. There was a mix-up, and most of their luggage was left on the dock. It didn't catch up with them for several days. But that wasn't the only problem. Their cabin had been assigned to another couple. This was straightened out but resulted in them getting a cabin that was not as desirable. The whole cruise was like a nightmare. My father had his camera stolen at the first port when they went out to explore the town. There was a kitchen fire that cleared the dining room one night. The mishaps even included my father taking a fall and coming home with his ankle taped up. When I picked them up on their return, my mother was crying and my father was very angry. Imagine my surprise at future gatherings when Father would entertain the guests with stories of that awful trip. If he missed anything, Mother would remind him, and they would go into gales of laughter, as would the company, at each and every mishap.

Many years ago, I was very active politically. One night, my club planned a huge fund-raising dinner for the men we were backing for state senate and state assembly. As part of the entertainment, a friend of mine, Sally, and I were to sing a song that was a parody about both politicians. It had a lot of verses, so Sally and I rehearsed endlessly.

The night of the dinner, we arrived with our husbands and mingled around during the social hour. No way was I going to muddle my brain when I had such a long song to remember, so I went over to the bar and had them fill my glass with club soda. As all my friends walked around laughing and drinking, I found myself repeating the song verses over and over in my head. I made small talk with a lot of people, just barely even hearing what they had said. I couldn't get that song out of my head. And when we all sat down to the steak and lobster dinner, everyone at my table was eating, talking, and laughing almost simultaneously. But I just sat there mentally repeating the song. I was so afraid I'd get on stage and forget the words that I was now feeling almost sick. I looked over at Sally, who was at an adjoining table. She was looking down at her plate, and I knew she was rehearsing just like I was.

Finally, the dinner was gathered away. We went backstage, and then suddenly, the dreaded moment was there. Sally and I came out on stage, and we were looking right down at the candidates, who of course had ringside seats. The music started. Our song went beautifully, and the crowd laughed at all the funny lines. In a few minutes, the ordeal was over. I never forgot that night. A few months later, I went to a Tony Bennett concert and instead of just appreciating his wonderful voice, I sat there thinking, *How does he remember all those words?* My one experience with show business was one of the more nerve- racking evenings I'd ever had, and I was miserable the whole time.

Sally doesn't live in Southern California anymore, and I only see her on her occasional visits. Yet every time we get together, sooner or later, that subject comes up, and we sit and laugh about that night as though our stage fright was very funny. This is just one more example of an experience that was terrible during its happening, but funny and enjoyable in its retelling.

There is a saying, "Comedy is tragedy plus time." Many comics build their entire routines around their poverty-stricken childhoods. Looking back from a distance, they can find humor in what must have been a terrible experience. Once more, it looks as though our memories are much sweeter than our experiences.

31. *Don't Bring Me Flowers!*

      I just said good-bye to some close friends who stopped by to see me. I have become one of those people who are whispered about. You see, I have a terminal illness, and no one can bring himself to mention it. Even my longtime friends that I have shared so many laughs with in the past have become humorless, sad-looking zombies. If it's the last thing they do, they will not mention that elephant in the room.

      Each time they leave, I resolve to write a pamphlet on how to act when visiting a friend who is seriously ill. And maybe, just goddammed maybe, I might even get out of this bed and nail it to my door. In my pamphlet, I will suggest that someone should teach a course in how to visit sick friends. Do you really think we want three-foot glass vases filled with long-stemmed flowers? Do you really think we feel better if you look gloomy and tearful?

I have an incurable illness, and in the beginning, I was hospitalized. The first morning, I awoke to find every table in my room filled with flowers. I thought maybe I had died already. When a couple of neighbors dropped by, they were both so tearful I spent their visiting time comforting *them*.

The noted writer Norman Cousins had a lot to say about this. He knew a lot about endorphins. I'd never even heard of them before I started reading Cousins' book. But apparently, endorphins are the little guys inside of you who are your body's natural painkillers. When you are in extreme pain, all the doctors do is give you stronger and stronger pain pills. But Cousins says never mind the pills; make this guy laugh, and his pain level will drop.

He conducted one famous experiment when he was in a hospital about a year before his death. He sent for some Marx Brothers videos, his favorite comics. Then before watching them, he had a doctor do a complete checkup on his body. After that, they put in the first Marx comedy, and Cousins began to laugh. And he laughed and laughed all morning. When he had watched all the films, the same doctor repeated the checkup, and he was markedly better.

This is what I want to put into my pamphlet—not just for my dear friends who just left, but to get through to the general public as well. I believe this theory. I believe that if we are surrounded by laughter, it may not cure us, but it will extend our lives and make them far more pleasant.

I can use myself as an example. I live alone, and my breakfast is cooked by a woman named Anna. She is a senior citizen who was an actress in her youth. While I eat, she tells me funny show-business stories. This was one of the reasons I hired her. One day, she told me of a play in which she played the slightly crazy daughter in a large family. They refused to put her in an institution, and most of the laughs in the play were when she would get away from them. She would run out into the street peeling off her clothes as she ran, happily singing a goofy song that started out, "I'm gonna dance in ma birfday suit." And while I laughed, she would get up from the dining room table doing her dance (minus the strip) and singing her goofy song. She was very funny.

I have another daily visitor, this one from a hospice, a sweet young girl named Maria, who comes in each morning to bathe me.

Most of the time, I keep myself so occupied I deliberately don't leave much time to think about my condition. But one day, I awoke deeply depressed. *Every day is the same,* I thought, as I pushed myself up and sat on the side of my bed. *I never get better. I never stop hurting, and I can't drive, which means I can't even run a simple errand by myself. I am too tired to go out to luncheons or parties with my friends. Even if I could go out, it would take me all morning to dress myself.*

I didn't realize just how depressed I was until Maria rang the back doorbell and I opened the door. To my surprise, I greeted her by bursting into tears. She quickly rolled my walker back to my bedroom and sat with me on the edge of the bed with her arm around me. She rocked me and said soothing words as though I were a small child, but I still couldn't stop crying.

Again, the back doorbell rang, and Maria left me to let Anna in. She must have told Anna of my depression on the way down the hall. Suddenly, my bedroom door burst open and in danced Anna singing and dancing to that goofy song. It was the last thing I expected. I began to laugh, and so did Maria.

Anna joined us sitting on the edge of my bed, and there we sat, three totally different people in terms of age, race, and background. We had our arms around each other, hugging and laughing.

I tell you this little story to show you what laughter did for me and how quickly it pulled me out of my depression.

George Burns and Bob Hope were just a couple of the many famous comedians who lived very long lives. And yet, think where they spent hours every night: standing on the stage of a theater telling jokes in a room so thick with cigarette smoke you couldn't see to the other side of it. Who knows? Maybe their endorphins were sitting inside listening and laughing at their jokes.

So I am suggesting that when you visit sick people, tell them the latest joke you've heard. Instead of bringing a beautiful bunch of flowers, bring them some really funny films to watch or books to read.

Try to take what time they have left and make it a lot more fun for them.

32. Whom Would You Pick to Deliver Your Eulogy?

Your eulogy should be a brief summation of your life. If you pick someone who delivers eulogies all the time, he may just get up and pontificate. He will try to make himself look good, not you. If you pick a loved one who has never done this before, he may be nervous and not tell the people some of the things you would like to have said. Are those really the final words you want to leave with your family and friends?

I thought about picking someone who would praise me to the point that the tearful gathering would think the world had really suffered a great loss by my departure. When he was through, there wouldn't be a dry eye in the house.

But wait a minute, do I really want a tearful crowd when I have spent so much of my life trying to amuse people? Maybe I should think more like George Carlin who wanted to go out with a laugh. I read that he requested that his tombstone read, "Geez, he was just here a minute ago."

There is just one way to see that everything is done to my liking, and that is to write my eulogy myself. And then who cares who delivers it? I led a rather unremarkable life, but what would stop me from writing about the life I might have led? I am sure the members of my writing group would be comfortable with this; they never believe a word I write anyway. So my only problem would be in deciding what I would like to be known for. What could I have done that could be considered unique and important? And then, I figured it out. I would like to have been known for my ability to turn a phrase—not just any phrase, but words that would actually become an important part of our history.

My mind wanders back through the years and stops with Franklin Delano Roosevelt. He was such a well-spoken man. But suppose, just once, I was able to help him. I could tell about the time when I was barely eight years old. I was living in Washington DC, and my class went to the White House on a field trip. And I, with my usual adventurous spirit, slipped away from the tour group and suddenly found myself looking through an open doorway where I could see President Roosevelt at his desk. He was scribbling onto a yellow legal pad, crossing words out, and then scribbling some more. He looked very frustrated and unhappy. Suddenly, he glanced up and saw me. I started to run, but he called out, "Wait, little girl! Come in here!"

I approached his desk, and he said, "I'm having an awful time. Even my speechwriters can't seem to help me! Our country is in such an upheaval, but I know things will get better. I want to say something tonight in my fireside chat that will calm everyone down. What could I say that would make you feel better?"

It was very clear to me. I looked up at him and said, "Sir, just tell everyone that there is nothing to fear but fear itself."

Well, I don't have to tell you what a great line that was. It is still being quoted to this day. But I never took credit for it, and I guess he didn't want to admit that he got the idea from an eight-year-old kid.

I was tempted to put in my eulogy that I was a perfect mother, not only in taking care of my children, but in giving impeccable advice for every situation they encountered. But I decided very quickly that that could be a big mistake. My children would be sitting in the front row listening to this, and I didn't want them snickering and nudging each other saying, "Oh yeah? When was all that impeccable advice?"

Instead, it would be safer to stick with taking credit for things that happened when they weren't around. Then they can't prove that I wasn't actually responsible for coining some of the most famous phrases in history. I'll just say that modesty kept me from telling them of this before, but I thought it was time that I let everyone know.

Here is another example of something that happened while I was still living in Washington DC. It was a great many years later, and I was now a teacher, taking my class on a tour of the White House. I saw President Kennedy on the back lawn playing with his children. Before the guards could stop me, I waved and called out a friendly greeting. He told them to let me approach and said, "Tell me something, do you or your students do any volunteer work?"

I shook my head.

"Well, don't you think maybe you should get more involved with your country?"

I said, "I never thought about it. But it's a good idea. Why don't you get on TV and talk to the students and say something that would really inspire them."

"Like what?" he asked, as though he had no idea where to start.

Again, the answer was so clear to me. I said, "Tell them, 'Ask not what your country can do for you, ask what you can do for your country.'"

He really liked that phrasing, so I said he could use it. I sort of wish I'd capitalized on it a little bit, maybe had some T-shirts made or something. But once again, out of modesty, I let him take all the credit.

And some things, I must admit, got away from me because I was so adroit at turning a phrase that I just didn't appreciate how immortal my words were, and sometimes, I just let them slip through my fingers. Like the time I went into a diner, sat at the counter, and ordered a hamburger. I was sitting next to an elderly woman who had also ordered a hamburger. When the waitress put them down in front of us, all I saw was a bun! I picked it up and looked at the skimpy patty inside, turned to the old lady, and said, "Where's the beef?"

She laughed and turned to a photographer who was standing behind her. She held up her burger and said to him, "Where's the beef?"

And we all know where that ended up. It was the most quoted line of 1984, and Walter Mondale even used it in one of his speeches in his presidential run against Gary Hart. Again, I did nothing. I let my genius for turning a phrase make other people famous or wealthy. But then, I have always been innately modest, reluctant to trumpet my abilities. But now that I am gone, or at least will be when you read this, it is time to unmask and let you all know how brilliant and talented I was.

My family and most of my friends will accept my departure from this earth. But I don't really know what to do about some of my friends in the Writers' Circle. Even if they see the death certificate, there are some of them who just don't trust me. In fact, there is one member who did not believe it when I was hospitalized. I'd had major surgery for Pete's sake, but when I came back, he swore that he'd seen me alongside the I-5 freeway in an orange jumpsuit picking up trash. I am sure he will look around at each meeting for weeks after my funeral, clearly expecting to see me walk in saying, "Gotcha!"

About the Author

Vivian Charlton was born in Berkeley, graduated from Oregon State University, and moved to Southern California in 1950. After raising her family, she opened her own real estate office in Glendale. When she finally retired, she joined several writers' groups and began to explore her remarkable writing talents.

Appendix

Vivian and Siblings

Vivian's sister
Phyllis

Vivian and Phyllis

Vivian

Vivian

Vivian's brother
Norman

Phyllis and Vivian

Vivian's Children

Left: Denise a.k.a. Neecy
Middle: Steve a.k.a. Tiger
Right: Jennifer a.k.a. Jaffry

Jaffry

Tiger

Neecy

Vivian's Grandchildren

Tiger's daughter Kelly

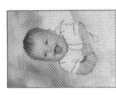

Tiger's son Rob

Neecy's daughter Katie

Jaffry's daughter Tera

Neecy's daughter Sarah

Jaffry's daughter Devin

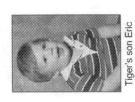

Tiger's son Eric

Vivian's Great-Grandchildren

Devin's son Patrick

Tera's son Tyler

Kelly's daughter
Autumn

Tera's son Mason

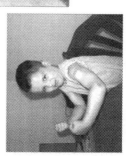

Rob's son Nathan